THE BONE WHISPERERS

THE BONE WHISPERERS

TWO WOMEN SCIENTISTS AND THEIR WORK TO CONNECT LOST LIVES IN BOSNIA-HERZEGOVINA

Taina Tervonen

Translation by Sarah Robertson

SCHAFFNER PRESS
TUCSON, ARIZONA

Library of Congress Control Number: 2024937817

ISBN: 978-1-63964-048-5

EPUB ISBN: 978-1-63964-049-2

ADOBE PDF ISBN: 978-1-63964-050-8

CONTENTS

2016

2020

To Sarah,

the little sprout who arrived during

the writing of this book,

to life that continues.

"It is a story of bones that one searches for,

It is like searching for dinosaur bones,

Except these are the bones of people.

We search for them because it is important for their loved ones.

When they are found, the families can bury them,

and just like that, they are no longer missing."

—ARMAND, AGE 9

PROLOGUE

It's 12:30PM, the lunch break is over. The team wrap up the remains of the meal which has been served on the hood of a car, for lack of a table. "Something sweet," she had said to me in English, offering me a square of chocolate as a dessert, adding: "we all need some of that here." Senem puts her mask back on, slips on a pair of clean gloves over the cuffs of her white overalls, adjusts her navy blue hard hat. I climb the mound of earth bordering the pit as big as a football field. Senem is already down below, far beyond the police cordon which I am not allowed to cross. The Bobcat gets going, the pickaxes are taken up, the work begins anew.

I did not know what to expect arriving here. Nothing had prepared me for the sight of a mass grave. Nothing, save a few archival images that I had come across in news reports here and there: the stories of survivors who could have ended up in the depths of this pit. But when it came to what happened when the earth opened and surrendered its past, I had had no idea. I was expecting horror, the unspeakable, the unrepresentable. The idea of a mass grave.

But a mass grave is not an idea, a mass grave is hard work. There was no place for ideas when confronted with this gaping hole, from which the bodies had to be dragged out before the winter came.

In the immense pit below, Senem is digging away with the rest of the team. They are forensic anthropologists like her or archaeologists and osteologists. They all wear the same white overalls, stark against the dark orange of the clay soil. The autumn rains have turned this into a sticky mud that clings to the investigators' boots and gloves when they abandon their shovel, dig with their hands, in movements that become increasingly adept as they get closer to the remains emerging from deep in the pit.

The man who had confessed to the police spoke about a number: 900. It was his estimation of the number of bodies buried here. He had driven one of the trucks used to transport the victims who had been killed a few dozen kilometers away during the first weeks of the war. It was the summer of 1992 and, as is often the case here, and as the survivors attest, it was hot. In village after village, they executed Bosniak and Croat inhabitants or imprisoned them in camps as part of the ethnic cleansing conceived and organized by Ratko Mladić and Radovan Karadžić. It cleared this region of Bosnia-Herzegovina well before the Srebrenica massacres that followed three years later.

The bodies that come out of the earth are surprisingly intact today. Senem usually handles skeletons, not bodies like these. The majority are complete, the flesh still attached to the bones. In this area, the clay soil delays the decomposition that will begin again rapidly in the fresh air, twenty-one years after their deaths. The smell of this death lingers everywhere, reaches deep into the nasal cavity, impregnating it for hours. At night, I can still smell it all around me in my room at the hostel.

Below, by the two red marquees that serve as shelters when the rain comes down too hard, a row of horizontal white forms contrasts sharply with the dark color of the earth. They are body-bags, on planks of wood laid directly on the ground. The bodies are numbered according to their order of appearance from the mass grave. The last one for today is numbered 109. The team have been digging for a month.

Each day, at 4PM, the bags are loaded into the hearse, a little navy blue van. They are taken to the identification center at Krajina, a morgue for the missing people of the war. It was here, one day at the end of September three years earlier that I had first met Senem...

2010

1

AS A KID, I WANTED TO BE AN ARCHAEOLOGIST

"**S**EE, THESE ONES FIT TOGETHER." Senem grabs hold of some vertebrae, "Look, the bones tell us about themselves." She assembles the skeleton like a puzzle, her hands rapid and precise, using practised movements: large leg bones arranged next to a pelvis, ribs around vertebrae, a lower jaw by a skull. I have never seen a dead person in my life. At the feet of the body that Senem is putting back together, a bright wool jumper has been carefully folded with shoes placed atop it, the leather stiff from years underground.

Lined up next to each other, the remains of seven bodies exhumed three days earlier are sitting on white body-bags on the concrete. The clearing away continues, as other remains, bones and vertebrae go into sealed body-bags to be sorted.

"There are twenty-two of them, all from the same mass grave," Senem tells me. Around me, trolleys with five shelves are lined up for several meters against the wall. On each shelf sits a body bag. How many in total are there in this immense industrial hangar?

I had landed in Sarajevo the week before. It is the second time that I am visiting Bosnia-Herzegovina. I don't know much about this country's history, apart from its war which ended in 1995, a war with a 110,000 dead, 30,000 of whom are still missing. They continue to look for a third of these, meaning they are still searching for 10,000 people. They are the ones who interest me, the ghosts whose return families are awaiting, in order to bury them. I had listened to relatives speak about the pain of this wait, the impossibility of grief. Yet the work required to identify bodies was not really something that I had considered. In Sarajevo, one of my contacts had mentioned Senem's name. She is a forensic anthropologist running the identification center in Krajina, a region in the country's northwest. When I had called her, she had explained to me how to come visit her: I had to get off the bus at the petrol station, follow the little road that passes through a residential neighborhood in the town of Sanski Most that then leads you to the Šejkovaća industrial zone. A morgue here? With my colleague, Zabou, we had walked along the road, doubtful in the early morning autumn fog, and eventually, convinced that we were lost, we had called Senem, to learn that in fact the building was right there in front of us.

I simply had not pictured it like this, a non-descript large-windowed warehouse opposite a cement factory.

To warm us up, Senem had made us a Nescafe instant coffee in the trailer that served as her office. I had barely swallowed a mouthful before she picked up her cup and suggested that we follow her into the hangar. In sweatpants and a leather jacket, hair hidden beneath a black woolly hat and only just thirty, she too did not fit my idea of someone running a morgue. It was as if life should have left its mark on a person before they had to confront death, or at the very least, clothed them in a white overcoat. Senem, however, entered the hangar as if she were arriving for a day at the office, coffee in hand. When she opened the doors of the large hall and I saw all the body-bags on the ground and on the trolleys, I hesitated. I wanted to protest, say surely you don't go into a morgue like this? Shouldn't you... well, I wasn't sure what, but Senem was already over the threshold, holding the door open and waiting for me.

I said nothing and went in.

"Before the war, there was a factory here," Senem tells me in English. "Then it became a morgue." She points to some photos taped to the wall. What sort of factory, I wonder, but I don't have time to ask her as she has already launched into an explanation of the images printed on contact sheets. One of them has the small, numbered yellow cones that you see at crime scenes, spread out across a pit strewn with bones. At the point of exhumation, everything must be photographed and recorded, she tells me. The position of the bones helps them to deduce if the bones belong to the same person and must be stored in a single body bag. Once at the morgue, the bag is opened, its contents washed, a second examination takes place.

"Sometimes the torso doesn't match the legs, or the age of the skull is not that of the pelvis. If you have any doubts, it is down to the DNA to determine which of the bones belong to the same person."

I listen to her. I try to retain it all, the bags on the ground, the trolleys, the bones, the DNA. The hangar seems huge to me. The roof is several dozen meters high, steel beams tracing out the graphic lines of its ceiling. The light enters a row of windows very high up, faint this morning because of the drizzle cloaking the neighborhood.

"The DNA allows us to determine a person's identity. Senem continues. "The deceased's genetic profile will be compared to others, obtained from blood samples from the missing person's family, which are all held in a database. And from this, we hope to get a match."

She runs through things as if she was running through a presentation that she has done countless times for visitors like me who have only ever heard the word "DNA" in a cop show. Senem actually looks like someone from a crime novel, with her leather jacket, cigarette in mouth, the piercing gaze and her serious manner, alongside the striking contrast between her almost baby face and the cadavers all around. She patiently explains to me what a "match" means: a genetic link proving a family relationship and hence an identity.

"The problem comes," Senem adds, pointing to another photo taped to the wall, "with the secondary graves."

In the photo, one can see ribs, part of the spinal cord, pieces of skull. A second photo by its side features vertebrae, a pelvis and femur bones.

"The upper part of this body was found at Jakarina Kosa in 2001. And here, in 2004, we have the lower part, exhumed at Tomašića, thirty kilometers away."

Near the end of the war, the perpetrators of the crimes set about moving the bodies in order to hide the evidence. Fifteen years later, the work of identification is now considerably more complex, the bodies rarely complete.

"Sometimes we have just a finger or a femur bone."

On the two-meter-tall partition dividing the hangar in half, tiny faces—stuck onto a strip of brown paper—watch us. They are the size of a passport-photo, sometimes even just cut from larger images, from family collections spared by the war and exile, showing serious faces or laughing ones, faces lost in thought, or with a cigarette in their mouth, a toothless smile, a military uniform, a childhood pout, wrinkles, a school photo, those hairstyles that take me back to my school years in the 1990s. They are the faces of all those who have disappeared in the Krajina region. They number more than 5,000.

"If we only have an arm, the pathologist cannot conclude a cause of death or create a death certificate, in which case we advise the family to wait. But the final decision belongs to them.

"And what happens if the family decides to organize a funeral and the bones are found later on?" I asked.

"Then we have to exhume an already-buried body so it can be made whole."

How many times can you bury a relative? I had never dreamt of such a question. I have no reference point for this world of the dead and certainly not this one, made up of violent deaths, executions and torture, the traces of which are left on anonymous bones spread out on body-bags or in the memory of families forever living in the hope of finding loved ones.

"The bodies here were practically complete," Senem says, pointing out white body-bags lined up on the ground from the most recently discovered mass grave. "These twenty-two bodies were not all mixed up together, they were laid out carefully in the grave." The exhumation took five days, which is a lot, "for such a small mass grave," she explains. "It meant we could take all the necessary precautions so I know that we will only need one DNA sample for each body, which is also better for the families." In her voice, you can hear her pride in a mission accomplished, a job well done. In fact, she says how much it annoys her when an exhumation is done haphazardly by untrained people. It means an increased time spent in examination and analysis, a longer wait for families simply because people had wanted to rush the process of getting the bodies out of the earth.

"Identification is like the full stop that a family can put at the end of a fifteen-year-long sentence," she says.

"All the more reason, if possible, to not replace it with an ellipsis," I remark.

"I know all about the waiting," she adds. "Before coming to Šejkovaća, I worked for a team collecting blood samples."

Her voice has changed, as if the official presentation is henceforth over. She tells me back then, when she began, she was just looking for a job, not a vocation. It was in this area that you could find work, in this search for the missing. As a result, Senem spent four years travelling across Bosnia-Herzegovina, Slovenia, Croatia and Sweden, looking for relatives scattered across Europe by the war. At twenty-one, she found herself on the frontline dealing with bereaved families. I ask her what it was like, she replies with an anecdote.

"One day, I had to question a woman who had lost her husband and six sons. Her DNA could have enabled the identification of seven people. Seven people, that is huge. I explained why a colleague and I had come. The woman remained prostrate and mute for three hours. We couldn't do anything for her."

When, in 2005, the then-coroner at Šejkovaća suggested she become her assistant, Senem did not hesitate. It was easier than listening to the families. She tells me that she prefers conversing with bones. She obtained a grant permitting her to complete her training in England at the University of Central Lancaster and which made her, in 2008, the first qualified forensic anthropologist of her country. She was very quickly appointed director of the center.

"I am good here, she says. I would never have imagined myself doing this job but it has become a passion. As a kid, I wanted to be an archaeologist. In a sense, it's what I have ended up doing."

Around us, the hangar is silent, the light has begun to penetrate through the windows, the fog must have cleared outside. I imagine Senem as a little girl, dreaming of archaeology. She was twelve when the war erupted. She never left her home, apart from two months in 1992 spent with her mother and ten-year-old brother in Croatia, near Split. Worried for his family, her father had sent them there. "It was nice, we swam all day long," Senem recalls. "Then in July, we were told we either had to return to Bosnia or leave for another country. They suggested to us Finland, Denmark or the US. My father came to get us and we returned to Novi Travnik, to our home. The next day, it erupted. It was hell for four years."

Standing amidst the rows of trolleys, she tells me about the years of war in Novi Travnik, split into two neighborhoods, one Bosniak and one Croat, who battled each other for four years. Her family, Bosniak who were settled in the Croat part, watched the fighting for weeks before accepting that they had to flee to the other side of town. "One day, some of my father's former Croat students came to tell us that they could no longer protect us. We had to leave our house."

What stuck in her memory the most from those years was the birth of her little sister. It made her so angry that she refused to speak to her mother for two weeks.

"I was mortified! I was fourteen years old, we were in a war with barely enough to eat and here they were having a baby!" She bursts into laughter, saying it is all fine now, that she adores her sister, with whom she lives at their mother's home. Senem is single and has no children, a consequence, perhaps, of this complicated work, she says. She puts her own memories aside when she works, but sometimes they surge forth unprompted, like the week before, when she had examined the body of an adolescent. She thought about the fear that he must have felt at the moment of death, facing his would-be executioners in the middle of the forest.

"I was thinking about it and my own fears came up. You think you are strong, that it won't get to you, but it's not true." Once, driving alone to Banja Luka to see a friend, Senem saw a cat that had been hit by a car. She burst into tears, had to stop, couldn't calm down for what felt like the longest time. When she got to her destination, her friend had wanted to reassure her, having experienced the same thing, working as well with the missing. She had been the one who had accompanied Senem to see the woman who had lost seven people and could not utter a word.

"You just snap," Senem says to me in English.

The sound of a machine comes from outside the building. "It's Zlatan starting his day," explains Senem. A man is getting busy with a hosepipe and a pressure washer. He is wearing a plastic apron on his clothes with the logo ICMP, the International Commission on Missing Persons. This is the international body, created by Bill Clinton in 1996, which undertakes research work on Bosnia's missing in collaboration with the country's authorities. It is also Senem's employer.

Zlatan's work consists of washing exhumed bodies, cleaning off the earth that sticks to their bones and clothes. He opens the body bag, deposits its contents into a large metal basket installed under a wide awning in front of the hangar, then turns on the pressure washer. The machine's hum fills the air, the water spurts against the metal edges of the wire container, pours from the grating at the bottom, streams onto the tiles of the floor, all mixed up with black earth. Under the jet, the dark form scrunched into a ball opens out, the colors become visible, a blue wool sweater appears. Fine plant roots are woven through the knit, impossible to be removed without damaging the garment. The twenty-two bodies were buried in a forest, placed into a natural cavity on their backs, eyes towards the sky, several layers deep and covered in stones and large branches, which took root over time.

Senem sees a respect for the dead in this configuration: "good intentions," she explains, concluding that the gravediggers could not have been the killers. "You don't see this kind of attention to detail for the dead when you have murdered them. They are tossed in, not lined up like this. Bodies are not always buried immediately, although when a body decomposes it smells bad, is hard to bear. Why would you go to so much trouble when you've just killed someone? Nobody does that."

Zlatan carefully lays out the sweater, places it on a drying rack, next to a pair of torn black underpants and white shoes. The clothes seem more human than the bones. These have been arranged on a large sheet of brown paper, placed over a body bag, a second one. A young woman is climbing a stepladder, holding a small camera to photograph them. She is called Bejsa, she is Senem's assistant. Zlatan takes a break, pulls out a plastic chair to sit, lights a cigarette. Senem gets one out as well. Her cigarettes are long and slender, she keeps them in the pocket of her black leather jacket. She offers me one; I don't smoke.

"More than anything, the mass graves we find today, are largely located due to confessions. It doesn't happen often though," she says, taking a drag on her cigarette. "We have been able to exhume these bodies because a man confessed to a policeman that he used to have coffee with. One day, the man told him about the mass grave, gave him the names of the people who had buried the bodies. The next day, he committed suicide. The policeman thinks that he had nothing to do with these particular deaths but probably had other crimes on his conscience. It seemed his daughter had big problems with drugs and alcohol."

This often happens, a personal drama prompts people to talk. Senem remembers a war criminal who came forward to confess after his daughter's suicide, another who started talking after his wife and children were killed in a car crash. "Something haunts them. In a sense, they need to redeem themselves."

Zlatan gets up after his smoke, Senem stubs hers out. We go into the hangar again, she takes me to the examination room, filled with tables covered in brown paper. This is where the bodies come after they have been washed, for a detailed analysis where each measurement, each fracture, each distinctive mark is noted. On the walls and windows, hang diagrams of skeletons, tables indicating the size of a femur according to age range. On one of the tables, pieces of skull have been glued back together. Senem takes out an A4 sheet, the form to be filled in for each case, designated by a code made up of letters and numbers referring to the exhumation site and the order in which the body came out of the mass grave. For Senem, replacing that code with a name is a relief, giving her "great personal satisfaction." She talks about an adolescent of sixteen, whose body she handled. For years the mother had gone around each mass grave opened in her region, in the hope of locating him. "She was searching for peace and now, at last, she will be able to find it."

I ask, in her opinion, how much longer her work will continue, where is the full stop that will complete her own work? When everyone is found, is identified? Senem sighs. I can hear the tiredness in her voice when she replies.

"DNA is a powerful tool, but it is not the answer to everything. Currently, we have four hundred and fifty cases. For seventy-two of them, the process has been completed, we can bury the bodies. For a further one hundred and four, we have an identity but we are now waiting for new pieces of bone from their bodies. Of the two hundred and seventy-four remaining, we have cases where we know we will never be able to identify their bones. They have been too damaged by time, bad weather and animals. And in each of the mass graves opened, we have bodies that we cannot find any matches for in our database, because either all the relatives died during the war or they haven't given a blood sample. For the time being, we are keeping them all here. But for how long, I don't know. And then you have the errors."

"The errors?" I asked.

"Yes, in the beginning, just after the war, when the mass graves were opened, the families managed things on their own. They would identify bodies by clothes or personal effects and for instance, while we generally know the site of opened graves, we don't know the number of bodies exhumed. Mistakes were made. We realized this with the DNA samples requested by the International Criminal Tribunal for the Former Yugoslavia (ICTY). The justice system required scientific proof of the identity of the dead, but clearly it was also proof that a deceased belonged to this or that community and was therefore useful information for their investigations on crimes against humanity. And so today, it can happen that the database gives you a match for a body that has just recently been exhumed, although the family has buried another body many years before. It's very difficult for the family but we must put right any errors that have been committed."

My earlier question, about when her mission might end, suddenly seems very naïve. Senem decides to answer it all the same. Concerned, she does make it clear that it is a 'completely personal' opinion, not to be confused with any official positions that her employer or the authorities might take.

"Honestly, as time goes on, I have taken the view that the objective of having everything identified doesn't make sense. The NGOs, the authorities, the ICMP, they all have good intentions but sometimes all we do is cause pain to families when we request a new sample from them or because we have located a new piece of bone.... We could come up with something else. It could be an ossuary, a memorial at the site of each mass grave with a list of people killed there, so that families could have a place to gather. Because what happens in five years? There will still be families searching and hangars filled with bodies impossible to identify. If we cannot satisfy the families or the justice system, what are we doing all this work for?"

But who would take on the task of telling families that the search would be drawing to a close? Fifteen years after the end of the war, the question is still too sensitive to answer.

"Come, I will introduce you to my colleagues, Ajša and Asmir. They are both case managers. They are the ones who manage the relationships with the families, receive them here to sign documents once the identification is completed."

Senem leads me outside, where the sun has fully risen, making me squint as I exit the hangar to go to the prefabricated building where Ajša and Asmir are working. I turn back to look at the white building, its details that previously had been hidden by the fog when I'd arrived: the corrugated iron roof, the rust on the door, the large windows, opposite, the prefab, the dog kennel, the hut for the police to guard the site. "A cigarette first," Senem says. She gets out a plastic chair from the entrance, lights up a smoke. I do not know it yet, but I too will become a part of this place.

2013

2

A MASS GRAVE IS HARD WORK

TOMAŠIĆA, NORTHWESTERN BOSNIA, OCTOBER 2013

The mist is everywhere. It envelops the landscape, the two houses that we have just passed. It blots out the horizon for two meters in front of the car, which advances in jolts to avoid the water-filled potholes. The track up the hill appears to be made solely for tractors and not little rental cars like our own, which any minute now, is about to get stuck in the mud. The team of investigators overtakes us in their SUV. Unlike us, they are fully equipped for this kind of place. Mass graves are rarely found in easily accessible sites. This one is located on the land of a former iron mine. Bodies were buried where no one would be surprised to see overturned earth. It must have appeared as an ideal solution during that summer of 1992. The mine had still been active a few months earlier, the mechanical diggers probably still in place.

Right at the end of the track, behind immense clods of earth displaced at the beginning of the dig, lies the open pit, its contours shrouded in the morning mist. The team is already getting changed in front of a canvas tent, set up nearby to store equipment. Senem has a routine: she pulls her hair into a ponytail, puts on woollen socks, a white protective suit, afterwards gloves on her hands taped down at the wrist to make them more impermeable. She wraps plastic bags around her feet to her knees for the same reason, puts on another bodysuit over the first, followed by rubber boots, a second pair of gloves, a mask and a helmet.

Three years have passed since our first encounter in Šej-kovaća. In the meantime, I have returned to the identification center to film scenes for a web documentary that I have co-directed with Zabou, the photographer who accompanied me during my first visit. The film tells the story of the village of Trnopolje, whose school was turned into a prison camp during the war. Over these last three years, I have listened to dozens of accounts of survivors who continue to search for their relatives, all disappeared during that summer of 1992. Senem again spoke to me about her work, but this is the first time I see her "on the ground," as she says, right at the heart of an excavation.

I had learnt about the discovery of the mass grave two weeks earlier, had hesitated at first. Was there not something morbid about heading off to such a place, given no media organization had sent me? Then I checked my bank account, called Zabou and sent an email to the prosecutor in charge of war crimes. A greenlight secured, I booked a flight. I had the sense that if I did not go, I would regret it. I wanted to know the significance of such a moment, when quite literally, the past has risen to the surface.

It is my second day on the site. Senem pulls down the hoods of her two bodysuits over her navy blue helmet bearing the ICMP logo. Only her eyes are visible.

"It's the only way to avoid the smell seeping into the fabric and even then, it doesn't always work!" she blurts out from behind her mask.

The smell obsesses everyone here. Yesterday, on arriving at the village where I am staying, a friend had told me about the site, and the first thing he mentioned was exactly that: the smell. As if that one word could sum up the thing that should not even exist.

Parked a few dozen meters from the SUVs, two diggers and a Bobcat are ready, their wheels and chains covered in the dried mud of the day before. The drivers carry around jerry-cans, fill up the tanks with gas, then climb in. The engines start, transforming the place into a world of building-site sounds. When I close my eyes, I have the impression that I am at my window in Montreuil, listening to the many weeks of roadworks on my street. The Bobcat slowly descends the slope which leads to the pit, while the diggers climb the sides to continue clearing the earth, to allow the team to search further over even a larger surface area.

Senem goes down to the spot which has been dug out the day before. I see her go into the depths of the mist with her colleagues and grab hold of the spades and pickaxes by the two red marquees, the only splashes of color in a landscape shrouded in a milky haze. I walk up and over the clods of earth that border the mass grave, which is encircled by a red and white police cordon, a sharp reminder that we are at a crime scene. The site is guarded by a policeman 24/7, and a representative from the prosecutor in charge of war crimes is always present when the team is working. His name is Eldar. He carries a large blue notebook in which he writes down all the day's information: the bodies brought out of the earth, the serial number attributed to each, the objects found in their pockets and the daily visits to the site.

I struggle to make out Senem amongst the eight white silhouettes that are busying themselves down below, all resembling each other, the majority with their hoods pulled up. The forensic pathologists cluster together in two's or three's, they pause, have discussions, put down their spades or pickaxes, scrape at the earth with their hands, take pictures and measure. Little by little, the sun clears the mist and I can make out the pit's contours. It is immense. The grave resembles a large basin, with different levels of excavation scattered across its bottom. Two silhouettes in white start moving agitatedly around a dark heap emerging from the earth, as a third goes to find a white body bag and unfolds it on the ground, in preparation for what is to emerge from the soil. A little further on, cones mark out new zones for digging.

It is not the first time that a team of forensic pathologists have dug at this site. In 2003, excavations had already taken place just a few hundred meters from here. At the time, they found around twenty bodies, then stopped searching. Some of the remains exhumed from this site were linked to body parts brought out of other mass graves thirty-odd kilometers away at Jakarina Kosa, where they were able to identify 308 victims in 2011. The forensic anthropologists immediately thought of bodies that had been displaced, but they assumed that the primary mass grave was at Jakarina Kosa. It turned out to be the other way around.

"We had known for a while there was an important mass grave somewhere around Tomašića," Eldar explains to me during the morning cigarette break. "That name would often come up in the discussions or speculations. But we did not know exactly where."

Then someone started talking. It was the driver of one of the trucks that transported the bodies.

"He was part of a group of suspects in our investigations of these crimes. He finally decided to talk, after a deal with the court. Let's just say in exchange for his confessions, he can no longer be prosecuted."

The bodies buried here came from several villages in the region as well as the prison camps. They would have most probably been transported here during the months of June, July and August 1992, "especially in July," Eldar says, by way of precision. Bullets found in the mass grave seemed to show that on-site executions took place there. The victims would have all been Bosniak and a few Croats, all killed by Serb militias and the Serb army.

"For the bodies brought by truck, they were people executed in their own villages. They left the bodies in the gardens and courtyards, and in the houses. That is when the other inhabitants started to complain about the smell. They came with trucks to get the nine hundred corpses and bring them here, to Tomašića."

How many trucks does it take to transport nine hundred bodies? How many return trips? Who oversaw all this? There is always somebody in charge to organize the transport, calculate the number of trucks, buses and trains required, or even the number of last cigarettes destined for those to be executed in some clearing, chosen for its proximity to a cave, into which bodies can be tossed. As was the case for another mass grave of the region, at Hrastova Glavica.

"We are now certain that this mass grave was re-opened in 1993 and its bodies were moved to Jakarina Kosa," Eldar continues. "As we have identified around three hundred victims over there, we expect to find six hundred bodies here. But it is far too early to confirm what it eventually turns out to be. That said, what we do know is that we are finding a lot of complete bodies. We are also finding sheets and coverings, probably used to carry the bodies, as well as gloves for the same purpose, all thrown into the pit."

A complete body is generally a clear indication of a primary mass grave. When human remains have been transported from one place to another, it is more usually body parts that are found, often all mixed up together.

"Why did they only move three hundred bodies?" I ask. "Surely if you are going to conceal a crime, why would you leave the evidence in place?"

"Probably because it is smelly work and no one wanted to do it," Eldar says, a hint of a smile appearing on his face.

I can discern a touch of black humor in his voice. He is used to having to reason in such macabre logistical terms during his investigations. He works at the Department for War Crimes in Sarajevo. This is all he does, war crimes. As for me, I am now pondering how many bodies you can fit into the bed of a truck.

Eldar continues: "After they reopened the mass grave here in 1993, they covered over the site with tons of earth, creating a little hill over it. When we began the excavations a month ago, we had to first clear the ground of a height of four to five meters of earth before we could get to the ground level of the time. We could clearly make out the earth that covered the surface. It was far darker than the original earth, which is more yellowish and muddier, a type of clay. It was only after we removed these many tons of earth, that we were able to start digging ten days ago. This is where we came across the first piles of bodies. The earth keeps the trace of all this: where it has been dug, the soil is darker."

Now that the mist has fully cleared I survey the landscape, a placid, valleyed landscape. It has bushes, some young birches whose leaves have begun to turn to the oranges and yellows of the coming autumn, and other larger trees, a little farther away. I imagine the place before the two diggers began to carry away the earth. A little hill built to hide what had been committed in this place, the way the bushes had grown over, giving it a semblance of normality. Yet the earth below bore the signature of the crime.

All day long, standing on the clods of earth, I observe the team at work. They scrape the ground, take the soil away in orange buckets, swap the size of their pickaxe, pull on something. It is the edge of a sheet. Meanwhile Senem has immersed herself in surveying. She spends hours taking measurements, as if involved in roadwork. The sun begins to beat down, she must be hot in those two bodysuits taped at the wrists, in material that cannot breathe. The covering has emerged from the earth, the hand movements around it now more deft. It is the contours of a man that the gloved hands make out, readying to deliver the cadaver from the soil. The investigators double up to get hold of the cadaver, a stiff mass that they place in a body bag spread out on the earth, after which it is taken to the red marquees and laid out on four wooden planks on the ground. The prosecutor writes a number on the white bag in black felt tip. The allocated code will serve as a provisional identity. Each body is photographed with the bag open, and in front of the bag, stand yellow cones with digits making up a number, along with a document in an attached plastic sleeve indicating the place of exhumation and the day's date: Tomašića. 8.10.2013. The first body to come out this morning has no head. It is wearing jeans, a blue sweater, its twisted limbs discernible, petrified into a position not by nature but by having been piled into a truck, then buried under tons of earth. It is body number 110. 111 has a black skull with nose and eye cavities that seem to fix me with a stare.

Before setting off on this trip, I had called a friend who had already attended exhumations because of her work. Celine is a lawyer specializing in war crimes and knows Bosnia-Herzegovina well. We had met up on the terrace of a Parisian café, just below where she lived, on the eve of my departure. She had sat opposite me and gone quiet for a moment. She who is usually so talkative. Then she said: "I don't know how to talk about this. They are images that will stay in your mind, which you can never erase." Her particular image was of a woman's scarf retrieved from the earth.

I think about Celine's words again as I stand here in front of the mass grave. I watch the team working, their methodical movements, their tired faces when they walk up for a ten-minute cigarette break, their bodysuits becoming more and more mud-stained as the day progresses. And I can see the scene twenty-one years earlier: the Serb army soldiers assigned to the task, getting to work around the mass grave. They too were just doing their job. The mechanical diggers were here, the shovels were here, the living and the dead were here. That same tiredness was here, the weary movements, the smell was here and the weight of the corpses. The mud was here. The same desire was here to go home after a day's work, take a shower and move on.

Perhaps this is the thought that will remain with me: that actions can seem so ordinary, that the work of some can, patiently, undo the work of others, the banality of evil but also the banality of good.

In the evening, I meet Senem at the bar of the Hotel le Pont, in the town of Prijedor, around twenty miles from Tomašića. She is staying there with the rest of the team during the excavation, to avoid the round trips to Sanski Moost each day. She orders instant coffee, I have a beer. It is the first time we can really talk since the morning. At the mass grave, she is focused on her work, is careful about what she might say. I am here in my capacity as a journalist, and communication in these kinds of situations depends on the prosecutor's office. She is not authorized to make statements to the press and has no wish to be singled out by the media. Zabou had wanted to take a photo of her in front of the mass grave and she had refused.

Seated at the bar, Senem explains why: "At each exhumation, there are officials who come and get themselves photographed in front of the mass grave, to say that they've come, that they care about it all. I don't want to be a part of that. I am just doing my work for the families. That is all."

Indeed, that very afternoon, a delegation had arrived in the company of the regional representative of the Missing Persons Institute, the state organ in charge of the investigation. Men in suits and ties got out of two cars and swapped their nicely polished shoes for work boots. They went down into the grave, conversed with the prosecutor's representative, listened to explanations and looked. Then they put back on their polished shoes and left. They had come from Tuzla and Sarajevo, we were told. In the pit, the work had continued during the whole time, a strange contrast between the visitors' smart getups and the team's dirt-covered overalls, the contrast between those who have their hands in the mud and those who make the statements.

"I don't know how I will manage with all these bodies at Šejkovaća," Senem tells me, lighting a cigarette. "What will I do about the smell?"

I think back to the big hangar. No kind of refrigeration system exists in the building, nothing to stop the Tomašića bodies from continuing to decompose. The site was never intended for these kinds of remains, but for odorless bones, devoid of flesh. We are in the beginning of October. The work of identification will take months and the victims will not be buried until the next summer, in the annual collective funerals for those identified over the past year.

"I cannot remove the remaining tissue to just leave the bones. I risk removing bullets or destroying other evidence. And it's not permissible as far as the families are concerned either, for religious reasons." I listen, the idea seems strange to me but I can only imagine that she is considering all options, even the most incongruous.

"Otherwise, we will have to refrigerate a part of the building, God only knows how. Or have refrigerated containers. But all of this is going to cost a huge amount of money and I don't know if I will even find a budget for it. I even thought about re-burying the bodies, once the DNA samples had been taken, and exhuming them again before July, for laying them in coffins and the funerals. Then I thought to myself that would not work. In a few months, not all of them will have properly decomposed. Can you imagine the smell, when you have to exhume them, prepare them for burial, leave the coffins out in the open in bright sunlight for hours, during the ceremonies? That wouldn't be possible for the families." I can clearly see the problem. The collective funerals always take place on the 20th of July, during the hottest weeks of the year. Senem sips her instant coffee, her face in deep concentration, no solution to hand.

"I said to leave the body-bags open at Šejkovaća, to help release the odor and air them a bit. Zlatan has begun washing the bodies, but it is just him. He can't keep up this pace. The poor guy, not sure how he will survive all this." she says with a sigh. "The only good thing I see in all this," she adds, is that a lot of the bodies are complete. And in this region, the families have all pretty much done blood samples. We should get matches easily. I have high hopes that the identification work will go quickly. Maybe a few months."

Another young woman from the team joins us. This is Esma, the archaeologist. She is the one who examines the ground over the grave to decide where it will be dug up next. She speaks perfect English, has lived in the United Kingdom for years and completed her studies there. When I ask her why she chose to come and work specifically in Bosnia, she says it is her way of saying thank you for being alive. It is the only thing she will say about her life. She prefers to talk about her work, the way in which she can read the ground: "I look for places where the color of the ground changes, often in a rectangle. Nature does not create that kind of regular shape. It is the traces of a mechanical digger every time. Sometimes we find marks, we dig a square meter, a meter and a half and we find nothing, we just see that the color of the earth changes back again. It probably means it's an area they dug up in 1993, when they planned to empty the mass grave and take the bodies to Jakarina Kosa but found nothing and stopped. Perhaps they no longer remembered the exact location of the sites. No one really knows why they didn't follow through with what they had started. Maybe it took too long, was too complicated. Or maybe they thought they were done. After all, it can't have been fun counting the bodies brought up by the digger."

Listening to her colleague, Senem drags on a new cigarette. "What I have not been able to understand," she says, "is the silence. There must have been people who knew. How have they managed to keep quiet all these years? When they moved the bodies in 1993, during the war, it was done at night. To do this, they declared a curfew over the whole route from Tomašića to Jakarina Kosa. People knew, they must have been aware of it, because they were all notified about the curfew. They saw the trucks go by. They smelt the odor, it must have been dreadful at that time. Why have they not spoken, since all this time? It's always the same denial."

In this region of Serb majority, everyone keeps quiet. No one brings up what happened, neither the executioners, nor the victims. Silence seems to be the price to pay to live together again. Survivor associations have a huge struggle to exist or be heard. I ask Senem if she thinks this will be the last mass grave of the region. She shakes her head, clearly not.

"It appears the bodies we have just found come from the villages of Hambarine and Čarakovo, from all those villages on the left bank of the Sana River where massacres took place in July, 1992. If this is confirmed, it means we still have victims missing from Kozarac village which they ransacked as early as the month of May in 1992, as well as the execution victims in Vlašić, during August, 1992. Where are those bodies? I don't know. We still have twelve-hundred missing persons in the region. Even if we find six hundred in this mass grave, the same again will be missing."

Hambarine, Čarakovo, Kozarac, Vlašić. For the three years that I have been coming to the region, I am beginning to master its geography, one of painful memories and new reference points each day. I associate each name place with a story now. Čarakovo for me is Sudbin's village. He resembles my brother so much that one day the villagers took me to be his sister. He says that he is one of the privileged because he found his father just a few years after the war, in the well where they had thrown his body. As for Vlašić, that is the place where they killed Velid, the cousin of my friend Mirela, when he was nineteen. It is also the place where they executed Rasim, the father of Nedžad, who featured in my web documentary. Father and son had been imprisoned in Trnopolje School, which had been turned into a camp, but only Nedžad survived. Today, he works in the very same former camp, now a school again. More than 200 men in the camp were executed at Vlašić, on the edge of a cliff in the mountains, their bodies left to fall into the void.

Korazac makes me think of my friend Ervin, better known as Švabo, "the German" because, apparently, he looks German. When the war began in 1992, like me, Švabo was nineteen years old. The war surprised him as he was bouncing a basketball outside. The village was attacked by Serb forces, cleared of its inhabitants, the houses were burned, sometimes with the families inside, and men were shot on the spot, others beaten, tortured and taken to the camps in the region, at Keraterm and Omarska. The women, the old and the young were forced onto the road, to walk the five kilometers to Trnopolje school-camp. Švabo survived because he looked younger than he was. In the camp, he could pass himself off as a teen of fifteen and was placed on the bus transporting women and children to the other side of the front line.

Once off the bus, he joined the Bosnian army, which was pretty much all there was to do for a young man of nineteen at that time. He spent four years there, clutching a weapon and afterwards a camera. He switched from one to the other when a friend killed himself in front of him, playing Russian roulette, just a kid pretending to frighten himself. "After that, Švabo says, I couldn't hold a weapon in my hands. So, I started filming." Švabo tells me that he still wakes up in the night sometimes, his sleep disturbed by scenes of war. He has his theory about it. He says that during the war, his body got so accustomed to the high of adrenaline, that now it is over, his body has to make up for it in his dreams.

Outside, the night is falling. Senem has finished her instant coffee and I, my beer. Esma has left to go and rest. As I depart the hotel for the streets of Prijedor, I think to myself that this is the strangest chat in a bar that I have ever had.

3

WHY DID THEY BURY THEM SO DEEP?

The next day, Zabou and I make a detour to go and pick up Nemanja, a young man who will soon turn thirty and will work as our interpreter. Nemanja is Serb. He lived a good part of the war years in Prijedor before his parents had to send him to his mother's family in Serbia. He was eight years old. Nemanja has agreed to help us because Sudbin has sent us, the one who looks like my brother, and because Nemanja needs the money. His mother is the sole breadwinner in the family. Nemanja has completed architecture studies, but apart from a few internships, he cannot find work. Being the interpreter at a mass grave of Bosniaks killed during the war is hardly his dream job, but it will do for now as he waits for other horizons to open up. His real dream is to leave Bosnia for Amsterdam, or somewhere else abroad. Here, there is nothing. Nothing at all.

I need Nemanja in order to talk to the relatives of the dead who gather around the mass grave. With the team and the prosecutor's representative, I can manage in English, but with the families, it is more complicated. Each day, parents come to look, say a prayer, hoping to glimpse a clue that leads them to their husband, their brother or their child.

It is also the families who bring food for the team at lunchtime. The survivors' association have organized themselves to ensure a hot meal is delivered to the site every day. They have also banded together to cover the rental of the second front-loader to ensure the work advances more rapidly.

When the relatives arrive on the site, the atmosphere changes. The mood of methodical work, of concentration to get the job done as quickly as possible, to get the bodies out before the arrival of winter and snow, the required detachment for the job, all seems suddenly swept away, only the raw pain of the survivors remains. The team's progress slows, they are distracted, and there is a silent reminder in the air: the dead do not suffer, that is the privilege and burden of the living.

For the lunch today, it is delivered by two women who arrive in a red estate car, their trunk loaded with provisions. They have tied scarves over their hair as the women do here when they visit a cemetery or mosque. They head towards the graves, use a corner of their scarves to cover their mouths and noses, as the smell always takes people by surprise. The prosecutor's representative greets them. He does it with every relative who comes to the site. He makes himself available, answers their questions. The two women stand at the edge of the grave for a long moment, listen to the explanations punctuated by gesturing. The older of the two crosses her arms over her chest, tugs at her grey pullover as if cold. She is crying behind her glasses. The younger one, in jeans and a black sweater, puts her arms around her, espadrilles stained by the orange-hued mud. Then the older one turns around and retraces her steps back to the car. It will soon be time for lunch and there are people to feed.

I have to force myself to talk to her. I explain to her, with the help of Nemanja, that I am a journalist. Would it be alright if I could talk to her? Yes, of course it is. She tries to contain her emotions. I want to apologize, tell her not to feel obliged but she tells me it is not a problem, gets a hold of herself again. She is called Mirzeta. She is looking for her husband, as well as her brother and son-in-law. They all disappeared in 1992, as did three of her sisters' husbands. Perhaps they will finally find them, in this place. She turns around to look back at the pit and the tears come again. "Why did they have to bury them so deep?" she blurts out suddenly, her voice choked in pain. "Why so deep in the ground?" Her eyes look tired. I am unable to tell how old she is, save to say her age is that of the suffering, which makes both young and old look worn out and broken. "Did you do the cooking?" I ask her. I need to lead us, physically, onto more solid footing, to feel the ground beneath our feet and not be washed away by the wave of pain engulfing the pit. "Yes," she replies, "with my neighbor we have made soup and bureks. Would you like some? There is enough for everyone!"

Mizreta gets out two large pots from the trunk of her car. She has also brought cutlery and floral-patterned china plates that she sets on a green plastic table dropped off by a restaurant owner the day before. She adds bread, bottles of water, soft drinks and cups. She serves large ladles of soup and thick slices of white bread, busying herself while her friend distributes the bureks, still warm and wrapped in foil. Once she has served everyone, she lets them eat and chat and leaves to perch on a corner of the back seat of her red car, the doors open. She lights a cigarette and smokes silently, her head rested in a hand partly covering her face. She stares into space.

Then she gets up again and comes over to us. "Don't you want a little soup too?" Women, all over the world, know how to cling to the comfort of a warm bowl of soup when the world disintegrates. I think of the little chocolate square that Senem had offered me, on another day: "something sweet." I watch Senem as she smokes with her colleagues, one of whom has stepped away to make a call while she laughs at a joke. Afterwards, they make their way back down into the pit, the plates and spoons are packed up, the pots put away in the trunk of the car. Mirzeta and her neighbor leave, the work begins anew. The Bobcats start up, the diggers as well. Esma has located a new zone to dig up, guided by the ground's color and patterns too rectilinear for nature. The Bobcat's shovel tackles the ground, digs patiently for an hour, one shovelful after another, gently, so as not to damage the bodies which perhaps lie beneath. Esma jumps into the trench to guide the shovel's movements, only her navy-blue helmet is discernible, her blonde ponytail poking out. Then she raises her hand for it to stop. A new pile of bodies breaks the surface at the bottom of the trench.

In the afternoon, I meet Fikret. We do not know each other but we have a friend in common, Seida, who works in a survivors' association, and has put us in touch. Fikret comes accompanied by a young couple, perhaps his friends. They arrive with a little boy of around eighteen months whom the father lifts out of the car fast asleep. He takes him in his arms and snuggles his nodding head into his shoulder. All three make their way towards the pit. Then the father stops and holds out the toddler for his wife. She stays back while Fikret and the young man approach the marker cone. The young woman's shoulders start to shake, her weeping eventually waking the little lad, whose serious eyes open to behold faces and a landscape that he does not recognize. He frowns in his mother's arms.

"I didn't lose anyone in this war,"the young woman turns and says to me in English. "I didn't lose a soul and here I am crying. I thought I'd be the one to come and support him but I am the one crying. And look at him, he can't even cry, he is in too much pain. I think of my child, she says, this child I gave birth to, and I think to myself: what if I had to come and look for you here? You don't bring a child into this world to have to come to a place like this. I can't understand it. I do not understand how one human being can do this to another human being."

Fikret stands at the edge of the pit, right up by the police marker, hands behind his back. It is not the first time he has come to Tomašića. He has visited the site several times since the beginning of the excavations, as he always does when he hears talk of a newly discovered mass grave in the region.

"Twenty years now I have been looking for my family. I come because there is hope," he says, in a very calm voice, which might seem devoid of emotion were it not for what his eyes are saying. He lost his wife, Minka, his son Nermin, twelve, and his daughter Nermina, six, all killed in the village of Zecovi in July 1992. When it happened, Fikret was not there. He was working in Germany. It is what saved him and he can never forgive himself. He came back as soon as he could, after the war, and ever since, he has done the rounds of all the mass graves.

He looks at the pit, greets the team. I think to myself that they must have all ended up knowing each other, he and the forensic pathologists. I think back to the mother that Senem told me about three years before, the one searching for her adolescent son and how she too would go and see every new mass grave, driven by this hope.

The little boy is fussing, he wants to be put down, walk on his own, has had enough of being in his mother's arms. She has stopped by us, has offered to interpret, leaving Nemanja at a loose end and to one side. Fikret looks at the little one, tenderness in his eyes. If his children had survived, perhaps he would have been a grandfather, would have played with a little boy like this one, taken him on his shoulders.

I ask him what he feels about the person who finally revealed the existence of this place, "I feel gratitude," he says without hesitation, "because once again I have hope I can find my son, my daughter and my wife."

"I can understand the hope but how can one feel gratitude in front of a mass grave?"

"It's my conscience that permits me to," replies Fikret.

"I am grateful to that man. If there were more like him, they would have already found all the bodies."

In the new hole dug out by the Bobcat, two members of the team are trying to free a pile of bodies all tangled together. The day before, Esma had explained to me the extent to which they were often intertwined, because they were first packed against each other in the bed of the truck, then pressed down under tons of earth for twenty years. "First in, last out" she had said, summing up the logic of exhumation. "When you bear that in mind, you figure it out, manage to untangle them."

At the side of the pit, a woman of about fifty, in a pink T-shirt and black cardigan, studies the work of the team. She introduces herself as Mirsada. "I am looking for a blue shirt. My husband was wearing a blue shirt when they took him away." Her eyes scan the whole pit. She has sunglasses in one hand and in the other, her black handbag, delicately wedged in the fold of her arm.

"He was thirty-five years old. We had three children. They took the oldest one who was thirteen. They were both locked up in Keraterm camp. They let our son go, but him, they killed."

Her eyes continue to search. "I have never been somewhere like this. I'm surprised, I wasn't expecting this." Below, the team dig, scrape, pound, a new body is placed in a white body bag. The bag is taken away on planks, photographed and numbered. The eldest son now lives in France. When he heard about the mass grave, he organized himself to get back here. He arrived the night before. He wants to see the mass grave.

Mirsada understands this. "I want to see the place where my husband has been for the last twenty years. I feel better now that I have come. Maybe because here there is hope. It must be that." Nemanja translates in his sometimes uncertain English. Later, he tells me that it is hard for him. Not the English but being here. The most difficult thing, he says, is to feel the gaze of the relatives.

"When they talk to me, they look into my eyes. It is hard

for me to think to myself it is people from my community who did this." He says, reflecting, "It would be a good thing if there was memorial at Prijedor for all these dead. After all, several monuments exist to the memory of the Serb dead, but nothing for the Muslims. It would only be right if there was something for them."

This is a weighty statement coming from the mouth of a young Serb from Prijedor. In town, you hear it said that the "Muslims" left of their own accord, that there were never any massacres, and certainly not any ethnic cleansing. The denial that Senem talked about the evening before at the bar is well and truly present, not only in the silence but also under the guise of revisionism. I am not sure that Nemanja talks about his little interpreting gig to everyone.

At the end of the day, a little green car parks next to the 4x4 pickup. It is Sudbin, the friend that Nemanja and I have in common. He takes out his work boots from the back seat. It is not the first time he has come, he knows all about how the mud sticks to your shoes. Sudbin talks to Nemanja, waves hello to the team and gestures a greeting to Senem. They all know each other through work. Sudbin is an employee of the Prijedor Association which brings together former prisoners of the regions' camps. He was one of the first people given advance notice of the discovery of the mass grave, right at the beginning of September. "The guys from the Missing Persons Institute called me and said: 'Sudbin, I have good news. We have found a mass grave and it's massive.'"

Sudbin bursts out laughing. "Good news! Can you imagine! I live in a country where a mass grave with hundreds of victims is good news!"

I first met Sudbin two years earlier, through Senem, at the Šejkovača morgue in 2011. He did not live far away, so we met there for practical reasons. It was a strange place for a first meeting, but in the end it was a simple and familiar point of reference for us both. Sudbin had told me about the summer of 1992, the summer when he was 18 years old. He was finishing up high school in Prijedor, listening to Nirvana and Freddy Mercury and dreaming of studying architecture or medicine. The school year had been strange. Right from the beginning of the war in neighboring Croatia in August 1991, the portraits of Tito which took pride of place in each class, had disappeared. The grades of certain students suddenly went down, for no apparent reason. The teachers took to giving nationalist speeches during lessons, referencing the need to protect the Serb population, who they said were under threat. More and more, fear and suspicion started to take over this town where different communities had, until then, lived together in peace. "Like a collective psychosis," Sudbin had described it to me.

During that winter, a parallel Serb public administration had formed, under the name of "The Prijedor Crisis Committee." On radio and television, they brought up the violence being perpetrated on the Serb population in Croatia. The memory of atrocities committed on this actual population during the Second World War was raked over. Bosniaks were accused of wanting to establish a Muslim state. In March 1992, while the country was voting for its independence during a referendum largely boycotted by the Serbs, the crisis committee's troops seized the only TV station in the region. From that point onwards, nothing could counter the propaganda: Bosniaks and Croats threatened the survival of the Serb nation, it had to defend itself. The distribution of arms to inhabitants in the town was just the final stage of a systemic barrage which had continued for months. For certain people, this was now about self-defence, not ethnic cleansing.

That summer, the holidays began earlier. Sudbin remembers one of his teachers wishing a great summer to his students with these strange words: "See you next autumn, if you survive!" Sudbin said he did not believe it at that time. All of this was completely unreal, even when they began to bombard the Bosniak villages on the other side of town, even when the rumors about Trnopolje school, the ceramic factory at Keraterm and the Omarska mine having all been turned into camps, began to circulate, and even when the town of Prijedor was locked down by Serb troops led by Ratko Mladić and Radovan Karadžić. Over the course of the summer, village by village, the region was emptied of its Bosniak and Croat inhabitants. The village of Čarakovo, where Sudbin lived with his parents, his sixteen-year-old brother and his sisters of fourteen and twelve, along with the neighboring village of Zecovi—Fikret's home— were encircled by Serb troops during all of June and July. There was no electricity, not much left to eat but no way to escape either. Then, on July 20th, the family heard gun shots coming from Zecovi. That night a few villagers who had managed to escape from the village came to Čarakovo. They talked about summary executions and bodies left in the gardens. Sudbin says that even at that moment, it was impossible for them to believe that it could be true.

Three days later, the soldiers and the police occupied Čarakovo. Sudbin was at home, with his mother, his brother and sisters. His father had gone to look after one of his fields. Armed men entered the family house, shouting at his mother to give them her money and her rings, after which they pointed at Sudbin and his brother, discussing them amongst themselves and saying, "What do we do with them?

"They can go to the riverbank!" barked the one who appeared to be the leader. It was only as he walked with his little brother toward the bank of the river where they used to swim— but now saw bodies floating in the water—that Sudbin believed his schoolteacher's words. He prayed that death would come as quickly as possible.

Sudbin climbs up the pit, his boots sinking into the mud. "When I came here for the very first time, the excavations had only just begun. I was with my friend Mirsad. He lost fourteen members of his family in July 1992, and they haven't found any of them. Can you imagine the hope this represents for him?"

Mirsad runs the association where Sudbin works. For better or worse, Mirsad tries to get this story out into the public domain, with demonstrations, actions and commemorations that ensure it does not sink back into the silence or the historical denial. He struggles. The day that I met Mirsad, in May 2011, just a few days after I first met with Sudbin, Ratko Mladić had just been arrested, after 16 years on the run. That day, we had all met at the association headquarters, a little office on the first floor of a building over a café in Prijedor. Sudbin was compulsively surfing online news sites. "My God, my God... What a great moment!" he would repeat in English, confronted with one image after another of the former general on his computer screen. "I am a victim of this idiot," he had suddenly said to me. "But I don't want to think that I am a victim of a Serb. I am the victim of a war criminal. Persecutors and victims do not have a nationality. There is no collective responsibility for war crimes."

In town, on the same day, nothing seemed to signal the news of the arrest. In the café, the TV showed the usual music videos, no one was scrolling the channels for news about it. No front pages featured the arrest on the new-stands, this history that everybody had lived through together, the Serbs, the Bosniaks and the Croats. Talking about it publicly seemed an exercise in collective remembrance that was impossible to surmount. Sudbin knows all about this: one day in town he happened to cross paths with the man who had saved both his and his brother's life. The man looked away and Sudbin got the distinct impression that it was fear on his face that he was reading. The last time they had seen each other was at the edge of the river on the 23rd of July 1992, as Sudbin and his brother walked towards the water. The man, a Serb colleague of Sudbin's father, recognized the two teenagers. "You turn around immediately," he had yelled at them, grabbing them by the hand and leading them towards the waiting buses parked by the roadside. "Get onto the last one. Absolutely not the first!" The two teens ended up in the Trnopolje camp, where a few days later, they were reunited with their mother and sisters. It was here, that shortly after, Sudbin learnt that the first bus was headed for the Keraterm camp, where all the men on board were eventually shot. On that one day in July 1992, 394 people disappeared in Čarakovo. Some of them are very probably in the mass grave at Tomašića, in this pit that we are both looking at, that I have been looking at for the last three days.

"I have always been lucky," says Sudbin. "I have always had guardian angels." There was the soldier who let him leave the camp with the rest of the family during a bus convoy taking women and children to the front line, although, being legally an adult, he should have remained a prisoner with the other men. Then, there was the bus driver who kept watch over his passengers to ensure that they had enough water and did not allow any soldiers to board the bus. The buses that departed the camp just after Sudbin's were headed towards the Vlašić Mountains, a place where 228 men were shot. And most of all, Sudbin says, he was lucky enough to find his father only two years after the end of the war in 1998. He had been killed in a field. The body had been tossed into a well, with four other men. They were able to bury him "just" six years after his death.

Sudbin turns towards me and asks, "And Nemanja, what does he think about all this?"

"I don't really know. I don't think it's easy for him. You will have to ask him the question directly," I tell him.

Sudbin shakes his head. "He is somebody who is very sensitive."

As we leave the mass grave, we decide to stop with Nemanja in front of the two houses situated a few hundred meters from the pit, along the track which leads up the hill. One can be seen from the mass grave, a little white house below. All three of us—Nemanja, Zabou and me—are convinced that we will be sent packing without a word, that no one will want to talk to us but that is still not a good enough reason to not try. I stifle a gasp when we come face to face with a grandma who has come out of one of the houses and Nemanja straightaway introduces us as "two French journalists who have come to see the mass grave." We do not stand a chance with this approach, I think to myself. Does he really have to say, "mass grave?" Could he not say "site," or "excavation" or "the work they are doing above," a euphemism to avoid the difficult word? Ever since I have started coming to this region, the silence has got to me as well. I am careful of the words I use, the subjects that I broach. I have found myself on occasion replacing the term "ethnic cleansing" with "the events," simultaneously aware that I need to keep the conversation going but ashamed of contributing to the negation of history. Each time, I have the impression that I am betraying friends like Sudbin or Švabo, who fight for things to be called by their true name.

The woman replies that she has nothing to say, nothing at all, and that she was here during the war but saw nothing, heard nothing, not any of it. I do not push her. Her husband arrives, elderly as well, then the neighbor from over the road, the one from the white house, who is a man of around sixty years of age, with a tattooed torso and a shaved head. I am expecting to be asked to get the hell out of there, but the neighbor begins to talk in German, says that he feels bad because of the mass grave, feels awful about the families. He is called Bore. He was not here during the war years, neither before or afterwards. He has lived in Germany since 1968 and only came for the holidays before returning here definitively a year ago, to retire.

Ten minutes after our arrival, we find ourselves in the garden, sitting under climbing vines that shade the sun and are typical of the local houses, talking with Bore, who by all accounts, very much wants to talk. He tells us about a phone call from one of his sons in Belgium, a month ago. "He asked me what was going on in Tomašića, what was the story? I had no idea. What story? He said: apparently, they found a mass grave in Tomašića. A mass grave? It was horrendous. I felt so bad. A mass grave in the place where I live. I thought to myself: now I understand what the people of Dachau or Auschwitz might be feeling."

A few days later, he saw the investigators' pick-ups arrive, followed by the cars of those who he was able to identify, without even having to ask them, as the relatives of the missing. They had come to see the site. At first, when the road was far muddier than now, before it had been reinforced with whole truck-loads of gravel to allow the convoy of diggers to come through, he had opened the gate of his garden and offered it to the families for parking, to avoid getting bogged down further up. He says he feels guilty. It was their eyes, he says, he feels guilty because of the look in their eyes.

Bore assures us he suspected nothing of all this before his son's phone call, but after the fact, he thought about the stories of his father, who stayed in his home during the war, in this house where Bore now lives. He had told Bore a story about how lorries would pass by the house, back and forth, for several weeks. "After the phone call, I remembered the story about the trucks. My father did not know what they were transporting and I did not ask any more questions," Bore says.

The elderly couple listen in silence. They too must have seen the trucks, smelt the stench of death exuding from the cargo-bays. They say nothing about it. The old grandpa gets up, "We can't just sit here like this, with dry throats, come, I will get the rakija." He brings out a bottle, the little glasses, a round for everyone, then a second. We must try the grapes as well. We nibble them from the heavy clusters that hang above our heads. When we get ready to leave, the grandma goes into her house and comes out with a jar of conserved peppers, the paprika pods of the area.

"This way, they will see we're not bad people,"she says in Serbo-Croatian to Nemanja, who waits until we are going back in the car to translate her words to us.

That evening, we go around to Sudbin's house, Zabou and I. It is my first visit to his home, the family house where they were driven out, and to which he returned to live with his mother and sisters, also both single like Sudbin. They came back a little while after the war, after having lived in exile in Croatia for a few years, afterwards in Czechoslovakia and finally in Germany. When it became a matter of returning to Bosnia, the little brother, the one who was sixteen years old when he had walked to the banks of the Sana River with Sudbin, said he didn't have the strength to do it. He went to live in the United States where he married a Mexican woman. They have a little boy who has never set foot in his father's country.

Sudbin offers us apples from his garden. His mother brings grilled chestnuts, followed by biscuits and juice, the low table of the living-room soon filling up with snacks. Here, hospitality is sacred. The large TV switched onto Eurosport is showing a soccer match, then we change channels for a German series. Sudbin talks about the trips that he has made, the ones that he would like to make and how the winter is coming and it depresses him. "It is the time of the year that makes you want to commit suicide in Prijedor, to hang yourself from a walnut tree. And yet when I go away, I miss this town."

My thoughts return to his question about Nemanja. I suggest that we talk to him together about the way they deal with their town's history. Sudbin seems hesitant but promises to think about it. The next morning, Nemanja tells me he does not wish to be interviewed. He has spoken about it with Sudbin, on the phone after we left. Ultimately, Sudbin does not want to talk about it either.

Later, doing some research on the internet, I come across a TV report by a journalist from Swedish television named Bengt Norborg. The images date from January 1996, barely one month after the signature of the Dayton Agreement which brought the war to a close. A Balkans correspondent since the 1990s, Bengt Norborg attempted to investigate rumors mentioning Tomašića as the site of an immense mass grave resulting from ethnic cleansing. He came to the place and questioned the inhabitants of the surrounding hamlets. The majority refused to talk, but one of them, under anonymity, alluded to the back and forth of the trucks and the diggers. Another spoke about a communal pit and executions. The number of a thousand people was mentioned.

Then nothing more for almost twenty years. I look at the images in the TV report, for the most part filmed from a moving car. They are of burnt-out houses, snow-covered landscapes, a man talking in the car, another at home, just a silhouette, so as not to be recognized. Is it Bore's father? Impossible to say. Once again, the silence enveloped the room after the journalists had passed through.

4

WHERE
IS
THE
PEACE?

Friday morning and we head in the direction of Šejkovaća. For three days we have been watching bodies come out of the mass grave. Zabou dreads what awaits us at the morgue, but I for one feel calmer. The dead frighten me less than the memories of the living.

It takes a few detours to get ourselves going, to take the right road. I think back to the first time that we came here, the route that we took on foot in the fog from the bus station. Today, the sun is blazing, we are in the car, and it is almost as if we are approaching the place too fast.

On site, nothing appears to have changed. The hangar, the trailer, the dog kennel, the hut belonging to the policeman who guards the site and recognizes us. We greet each other with a smile. Ajša meets us, she remembers who we are too.

"You are the only journalists to come for now, it would be nice if the Bosnian press came as well!" she says.

There is a touch of bitterness in her voice, a little despondency as well. She offers us each a mask in order to go into the hangar, which I accept without hesitation. The doors of the morgue are wide open and the smell of decomposition is detectable even from the outside. I am frightened that once in the interior, with more than a hundred bodies, I will find it unbearable. Ajša looks like she is thinking the same thing.

"How can we work here?" she asks, accompanying us into the hangar, as if she is talking to herself. "How can we breathe?"

It is not the first large mass grass to be discovered, she explains, but they have never had to deal with bodies in this state.

"To give an example, at Stari Kevljani, it was just bones. There was not this smell. We have never known anything like this," she says, sighing. The Stari Kevljani mass grave, discovered in 2004, contained the remains of 456 victims.

The hangar has been arranged differently in order to accommodate all the bodies that come and will keep coming. The trolleys with five levels have been pushed against the walls to free up as much space as possible. The wall with the photos of the missing, previously separating the hangar in two, now separates one area for the washed bodies and another for the newly arrived corpses, still in their earth-stained body-bags. There are dozens of them laid out on the ground, the length of the walls.

On the other side of this wall of the missing, washed bodies have been laid out on examination tables or just on the ground, on brown paper. Clothes in rags hang drying on clothes-horses, a pair of Levi's with a black belt, leather moccasins of the same color. Next to human remains laid out in anatomical order, are personal effects found in pockets, objects that have outlived their owners. A wallet, some faded photos, a watch that has stopped. A bracelet. An old bank note in deutschmarks, a currency that

has not existed for thirteen years. A ring around a finger, on a mummified hand with nails and skin clearly distinguishable. Next to a red-checked shirt, a tuft of hair has been laid out.

All that is tangled up in the mass grave, soiled by the earth, is washed, sorted and organized here. The bodies speak a language of their own, telling the story of what happened to them by their final frozen position, this one all curled up, that one, feet twisted inwards, the toes facing each other and touching. I find it hard to bear the odor, even with a mask. Or perhaps it is simpler to focus on the smell rather than what I am looking at.

I can hear the sound of the Kärcher pressure washer outside, that hum that I can now recognize. When the Kärcher dies down, the birds can be heard singing, the sound echoes under the roof, they must be entering through the large windows and the big open door. The birds that sing amidst the dead – the second image that will stay with me.

Under the awning, Zlatan washes the bodies, as before. He undresses them by cutting their clothes with scissors, places the body in the metal basket, starts up the Kärcher. The mud runs to the ground, the flesh sometimes coming away under the powerful jet which usually only washes bones. Dealing with these bodies still in the process of decomposition, the tool seems more violent than previously. A leg remains stuck in a black boot, impossible to separate. One by one, Zlatan removes the remains from the metal basket, places them on brown paper spread over a white body bag on the ground, then moves onto the clothes. A pair of trousers, underpants, shoes. Asmir arrives, he has put on a white bodysuit and a mask to help Zlatan with the body-bags, too heavy to handle alone. Together, they carry the washed bodies inside, each holding one end of a bag, delicately, so as not to drop what it carries, then they come back out with a new bag. How many corpses does Zlatan wash a day? For two weeks the bodies have been arriving at Šejkovaća, very soon it will be 150. If there are nearly 600 in total, it will not end anytime soon.

Leaving the hangar, I come across a group of women in front of the trailer. I recognize Mirzeta, the woman who brought the lunch to the mass grave the day before, along with her neighbor. They are accompanied by another woman and a young man. We say hello, give each other quick smiles, it is all we can do without Nemanja's help. Mirzeta and the two other women go into the hangar. The young man stays outside, turns towards me, speaks in English. He tells me that he is Mirzeta's son-in-law, his father disappeared as well, in 1992, but he was lucky enough to find him in 2005. Always this word that recurs: luck. Those without luck have only hope.

"I live abroad now. I was fourteen when it happened," he says, "I remember it all."

I do not probe further, he looks tortured by these newly awoken memories. I can see pain written all over his face, the pain of remembering, of absence, of being here today, once again outside a morgue in search of yet more bodies. He says one of the two women accompanying his mother-in-law lost her three sons, she has found two, but is still looking for the third.

"What can you say to this?" he asks me. "There are no words. Only the images speak."

And yet, he himself will have no part of them, these images. He does not want to go into the hangar, did not even want to when it came to burying his father. "I want to keep the image of my father as he was, I do not want to see what is in there." No question either of going to a mass grave. His distress is such that I attempt some awkward words of comfort. "I hope that in the end, there will be peace."

He looks me straight in the eye and throws my words back at me: "What peace? Where is the peace?

"You have children with your wife?" I ask him gently.

"Yes, two. They are two and five years old."

"Do you think that one day, you'll talk to them about it all?"

"I don't know. One day, maybe they will ask me why they don't have a grandfather when all their friends do. Then, I'll explain it to them. I don't want to teach them hate but I must be able to tell them the truth. It must be done."

"Perhaps peace can be found in your children."

When the little group leaves, Ajša shakes her head.

"Every day, the families come. It is hard to understand why, because no one has been identified yet. We still have a few more months to wait for that. But I imagine they need to come, to do something. Anything is better than just sitting around, arms folded and waiting. That is why they bring food to the site for lunch. So, they feel they're doing something." She looks out towards where the car has just disappeared down the main road, lost in thought.

"Their pain, I know all about it," she adds. "It's mine as well. I lost my mother and my husband in 1992, in Prijedor, so I know what that is. I know what they're living through, I know what to say to them. I was lucky, I found my husband as soon as 1999."

Always this luck. I think back to the young man's question. Where is the peace when being lucky is being able to bury your loved one? After the war, Ajša's father rebuilt his house in Prijedor but when he passed away, his daughter did not want to move back. "Too many bad memories." She prefers the town of Sanski Most, populated with the Bosniaks returned from exile after the years of war. For the last twelve years, she has been working with the missing.

We head back to Tomašića at midday, under a radiant sun. The sky is a deep blue, over corn fields ready for harvesting, the dazzling light making all the colors even more vivid. We drive along little country lanes, a shortcut, as houses, fields, more fields, people, a dog asleep by the roadside, pass by. The villages resemble each other, Serb or Bosniak regardless, fields are fields, houses are houses. The only distinctive sign, which is unmistakable, is the presence of a minaret or an Orthodox church's bell.

It is only as I approach the mass grave, and once the car is parked, that, for the first time, I really study the surrounding landscape. Going up the hill, one can catch a glimpse of a lake in the valley below, encircled by a wood. The sun is reflected in the water and makes it shimmer. It seems that in the summer, people come to swim and fish there. I walk along the little track bordered by young birches leading to the pit. The autumn light accentuates the color of the leaves. It is beautiful.

At the mass grave, the team seem be slowing down, already anticipating the coming weekend, time with family, back home. To make sure nobody stays too late, work finishes up earlier on Fridays. Those who live in Sarajevo will still have five hours of road ahead of them. I scan for Senem, but I do not find her. During the cigarette break, Esma explains that in the morning, there was an accident: Senem slipped on the side of the pit and fell, a drop of more than three meters. "It's alright, she just broke her arm, but we were all very scared," Esma says.

I wonder what must have been her explanation to the emergency services: "I injured myself falling into a mass grave?"

At 3PM, the team pack up to leave. A grey tarpaulin is pulled over a pile of bodies still in the ground, a makeshift shroud before the work starts again on Monday. The exhumed bodies are loaded into the rented Doo Huskić hearse which sets off for the final transfer of the week. Boots are swapped for sneakers, the white coveralls and blue plastic gloves are thrown onto a fire made with wood gathered from around the pit. The 4X4s set off, the week is done, with only the policeman who guards the site remaining, watching us out of the corner of his eye as Zabou takes a final picture of the site, while I record the sounds of the place now that the excavators have stopped. I hear the wind blowing the orange-hued leaves off the birch trees, whirling them down towards a ground of the same color, I hear the dog barking in the distance, I hear the last cracklings of the dying fire.

It will be the third image to stay with me: nature's quiet patience as it regains dominion over the places of even the most unimaginable horror.

Saturday morning, we head for Sanski Most to see Senem. She lives on the edge of the town, in a residential neighborhood with buildings painted in light colors, not far from Šejkovaća, in an apartment shared with her mother and her little sister, aged seventeen. Senem greets us with a smile, her right arm in a cast. Her mother is there, it is the first time I meet her. She brings coffee and snacks, places juice on the living-room table.

I look at them both, there is always something touching to see an adult next to their parent, one can guess the child they once were, get a sense of something of the bond forged by years of shared intimacy. With a large headband in her hair, her hoodie and tracksuit bottoms, Senem has something of a teenager about her, accentuated by being at her mother's side. The latter shakes her head when her daughter tells us about the accident, how the earth fell away beneath her boots, the fall, the fear of landing on her head, how she put her arm out to protect herself.

"As I was falling, I thought to myself: no, this cannot be happening, I cannot die in a mass grave!"

At Prijedor's hospital emergency room, everyone guessed where she had come from due to her muddy outfit. She got the impression that it made the doctor ill-at-ease. Even if no one talks about it, everyone knows the excavations are taking place. It is perhaps what is the strangest about the silence: things are so evident, so present, that a crazy amount of energy must be expended to keep them hushed up, to brush them under the carpet, behave as if nothing has happened.

The silence is also present with the victims for that matter.

Having arrived in Sanski Most as a high school student, it took years for Senem to understand what had happened in the Prijedor region, just thirty kilometers from here. It still surprises her.

"Nobody spoke about it! Among my classmates, several people had lived through the ethnic cleansing. But they never spoke about it. It was only when I began to work with the blood collection team that I understood."

Senem often evokes the silence, the silence of the persecutors and witnesses that makes her angry, while that of the victims she handles betters. I imagine when you spend your days arranging vertebrae or reconstructing a skull shattered by a bullet shot from point blank range, putting order into the tangible evidence of execution and torture, your hands immersed all day in the past, it becomes increasingly difficult to accept that others can remain quiet, whether to deny history or guard against their own memories.

For me too, the silence is disturbing. It infiltrates everything, from public places to the intimate heart of families, stops parents telling their children their story, turns the pain of memories into nightmares, headaches or violent outbursts. Right at the beginning, I tended to believe that talking was the only way to ease the pain, for grief to happen. But the more I come here, the more I listen to my friends and acquaintances, see how they live, the more I wonder if silence is the price to pay to survive. Everything in its own time. Maybe the time for talking has still not yet come. And what would be set free with this talking? Ultimately, no one wants a society where people walk around with their bad memories for all to see.

Senem talks to me again about the work on the mass grave, about how all her colleagues have a direct link with the war. Either they stayed and lived on the frontline, or they left and lost family members. Bejsa, the young assistant from Šejkovaća, originally comes from Čarakovo, Sudbin's home village, decimated in 1992.

"I asked her if she was still looking for family members," Senem recounts to me. "She told me just some of her distant cousins were still missing. I'm so proud of her. She manages to stay very professional when confronted with all this, at the site." She explains this to me in her capacity as head of the team, her concern for her colleagues apparent, her face grave and serious. I wonder what would happen if when in the pit, a colleague working alongside her was searching for a close relative. Would she suggest that they take a break, a day off, even though there are barely enough of them already to do the work that needs to be done?

"For me, the hardest thing is the smell," she adds. "It immediately reconnects you with the past. It's the smell of a relatively recent death. You open the mass grave and because of that smell, it is as if it has just happened, as if they only died two days earlier."

I try to imagine this fragile edifice of recollections, the sense of stumbling on one memory, which sets off another. Trying to barricade yourself from the past seems an impossible endeavour, a kind of labyrinth.

"At first, I did not question my work that much," Senem says with a sigh. "It was just a job, a salary at the end of the month. But with the years, slowly, it has become more and more difficult. I can no longer stay as detached."

"Do you sometimes talk to a psychotherapist on the team?"

"We can. It is part of our employer's health coverage. But I don't think everybody is doing it. Certainly not me."

"Do you think you always have to be strong?" I push further.

"I don't really think about it in those terms. But when you ask me the question like that, I'd answer you, yes. You do have to be strong, always. I do not allow myself to be weak. Sometimes, I think about completely changing my job. I would like to grow medicinal plants with my father. He is about to take his retirement and move to the countryside, there is plenty of exploitable land around. I even have a contact in a pharmacy, someone who makes plant remedies and lacks the raw material. It would be a completely new project for me. I don't know the first thing about it, but I think to myself I could make it work. If I managed to run a project like the Šejkovaća morgue, why not this?"

"Do you ever think about a family life, having children?"

"It happens. In fact, when you came to Šejkovaća the first time, three years ago, I thought about it a lot, I spoke about it all the time with my friends. I suppose all women go through this stage. I even thought about having a baby on my own. Then the moment passed. I thought to myself the most important thing, for the time being, would be to have my own life, in my own apartment. I didn't feel ready to take on the responsibility of a baby alone."

In the afternoon, for the first time, Senem will talk to me at length about her own memories of the war. She tells me about the time a sniper shot at her, another time when she broke her leg, the journey to the hospital on the other side of town, the massive detour by tractor through the forest, then on a horse, piggyback on her mother, even hopping along on one foot, to avoid crossing the front line. "But all this, I don't know how to explain it... you forget about it after war. You no longer think about it. Years later, one evening, my mum was wondering what she was going to cook for dinner, and I asked her: how did we manage during the war? And we both had to think about it together, to try and remember."

Senem's mother, who had been in the kitchen, joins us in the living-room, she listens, adds details, tells the story, in fits of laughter, of Senem's furious reaction when she learnt that her mother was expecting a baby, her sullen anger lasting 15 days. "It's true, her mother explains, my two previous pregnancies had been very difficult and they warned me that I might not survive giving birth a third time. When the time came, my husband negotiated with the Croat major to let the car through taking me to hospital… And well, now everything is fine. Senem adores her sister!" and she bursts out laughing again.

When it is time to leave, the moment of goodbyes, I find myself alone with this woman in her fifties at the entrance of the apartment. She addresses me in a considered way, weighing her words, as if she needs to convey an important message: "You are lucky to live in a normal country, a country without war. Because the war changes us all, every one of us. One way or another. After the war, it was still a war, to find a way back to some kind of normal life, an everyday life."

Back in my own daily life, in the Paris suburbs, taking the subway, dealing with kids' homework, making the evening meal, article deadlines, complicated finances at the end of the month, not always straightforward shared care, the words of Senem's mother often came back to me. It was the first time that the thought had occurred to me, the idea that avoiding war was not the normal state of things but a privilege, a piece of luck, as it was to find one's missing relative and bury them in a post-war country. I am lucky indeed.

2014

5

THE SALT OF THE EGYPTIANS

The train had made its way across the Croatian country-side, then stopped at the frontier. Locomotive change, passport control, custom officers on board. I am alone in a cabin for six. The wind gusts into the compartment through the open window when we gather speed again, tickles the nape of my neck, relieves the suffocating July heat. The landscapes file past progressively quicker by my window, I know them by heart now. The river where the train tracks follow it for a moment before pulling away, the pine forests all around. In a few hours, I will be in Prijedor again. Hello, Prijedor, I will say to myself, hello, to the town that is so silent about its past that you would think it has no memories were it not for the air so utterly charged with them that you feel you are breathing them in with every step.

For the first time, I am coming back alone, with no clear purpose, if only to be present on July 20th, the day of the funerals. While I was having breakfast on a café terrace in Zagreb, the list of 284 names posted by Sudbin appeared on my Facebook news-feed. For the first time, I felt a heavy weight bear down on me. Until then, I had just been an observer. I thought again about Rasma's words, this woman of about sixty whom I had filmed for my web documentary, her words when I had gone to see her in her little house surrounded by a vegetable garden to bring her a DVD of the film: "Now, we are the same family, even if we don't share the same blood." Seated in her always immaculately tidy living-room, she had officially made me a part of this story, her usually smiling face now a picture of seriousness. My blood will never have to identify anyone, I have that privilege. I look at names that I recognize, Duratović, Hopovać, Musić. How can they weigh so heavily on me, like a lead weight bearing down on my back as I read down the list of those to be buried in five days. Nearly all of them are victims of Tomašića.

At Trnopolje, the Maroslić home is as welcoming as always, a house with wide-open arms. Emira and Mehmed have left to go see their daughter Mirela in Tuzla. Their second daughter, Medina, will arrive later, for the summer holidays. I enter with the keys entrusted to me, I recognize the familiar sofas in the kitchen, the coffee cups. I put down my suitcase and backpack, settle in and get comfortable on the terrace to write. The two cows in the adjacent field are lowing, a flock of birds chirp in the neighbor's tree. I hear an apple thud on the grass, one of those red apples that Mehmed gathers in the garden and makes into a little pile at the base of the tree. My phone rings, it is Emira, she asks if I am not too scared to be all alone in the house. No, it's fine, don't worry, I assure her. They will return home in a few days and will be there for the funerals, she tells me.

Sitting on the terrace, bare feet enjoying the cool tiles, I think about Emira and Mehmed, their daughters, the hours spent in this house over the last four years, talking, laughing and playing cards. When I began the web documentary in which Mirela featured, Emira did not want to talk about all that had happened during the war. "Too much pain, what's the point?" But she hosted us in this house, she fed us, and at each meal, she asked us to tell her about our day. This is how the stories came, between the main course and dessert, or during the card games after dessert, stories that burgeoned with each passing day. Mirela had never been party to these stories before, although her thirst to know about them had been intense, to not have to imagine it all. She listened to her mother telling us them, and in the end, she was the one who asked the questions.

The light is fading, the birds have nearly fallen silent, thunder rumbles in the distance. I await the call to prayer which will mark the breaking of the fast, a sound that takes me back to my childhood in Senegal. When the first notes of the call resound across the countryside, I close my eyes and listen: the muezzin, the sheep bells, another falling apple. I never knew that you could listen to apples falling. Now, I know.

Tomorrow, I will go and see Senem in Šejkovaća. "We are preparing the bodies at the moment," she had said to me in a text as I arranged our meeting. Her words had the force of habit in them. She prepared the bodies every year.

The next day, I begin my journey towards the dead by taking the taxi waiting for me in front of the Trnopolje school. Or rather: I begin my journey as I step out of the Maroslić's house, locking the door behind me. Or maybe it was two days earlier, taking the plane from Roissy-Charles-de-Gaulle.

No. My journey to the dead began when the dead came to me at the edges of the mass grave. When I made the decision to come to the mass grave. When the first news about the mass grave reached me. That was the point when the journey begun, but I had not known that it would lead me here, to this day.

I come out of the house, it is just after 8AM, and the sun bears down on my head already, making me realize that my cap is at home, left in Montreuil. I take Mirela's route, the little path that leads to right in front Rasma's house, with the school a few dozen meters ahead on the left. I walk in the grass, the sun beats down but has not had time to burn away the morning dew. I feel the humidity penetrate my canvas shoes, reach my skin. The snails and slugs have come out, blue flowers, and yellow flowers and white ones border the path. I must ask Mehmed what they are called. In my mind I go over the words of Mirela, who had shown me this childhood way to her school. "I went across the fields..." I think about the story of this war that appeared out of nowhere, but was foreseeable, and I think that war can suddenly loom from anywhere, at any time.

The day before, after getting off the train at Prijedor, I had stopped by Sudbin's office. I had brought him spices from Paris. He talked to me about cooking: "It is almost a religious thing, taking everything that God gives us, and making a meal with it, focusing on that, forgetting everything else—that is cooking."

"For me, it's walking." I had replied.

Sudbin had begun his day with a phone call from a man who, this year, was about to bury his six brothers. Telling me this story, he was shaking his head, with that look that I now recognized so well, a look that both said: "How crazy is this! and "How could this happen to me?"

"This is the best time of year because everyone comes back for the summer, but it is also the worst because they all come back for the funerals," he added. We come back to honor the dead. Maybe it makes us stronger."

In the bus taking me to Sanski Most, I think about Fikret again. Did he find his wife and children? I remember his hope at the edge of the mass grave, his dignity, the sadness that he wore like a garment that he never took off. I need to read the list of names again.

Senem comes to pick me up at the bus station. She has her mobile phone glued to her ear, drives with one hand, seems pre-occupied. Blue top, pink trousers—a work outfit that I have not seen her wearing until now.

"It's good that you came. You are loyal to the victims," she tells me after coming off her phone. I am grateful for this description which sums up something that I have not been able to put into words myself: the need to come and pay respect to the dead who I have watched emerge from the earth. To witness their lives in death, this strange parenthesis of time between the moment of their exhumation and the moment of their burial.

On site, I find again the trailer, Ajša in front of her computer screen. Nothing has changed. Ajša takes my bag and puts it on the table, pointing out the stale carpet dotted with stains. "It's dirty on the floor!"

Senem gets me a coffee and takes me inside the hangar. I had forgotten how much this morgue is like her home. "You can come in with your mug," she tells me, but I have to put my cup down. For me, this place is not an everyday place. It is the fourth time that I have entered it. I know what awaits me inside, I no longer dread it like the first time. But the more I come, the more I feel the need to somehow collect myself. Even if it is just to put down my coffee cup before entering.

Inside, there is the sound of ventilation and the air seems cooler.

"Oh, you finally got a cooling system!"

"No, far from it, it's just some fans and on top of that, we have just the one that works, up there."

The smell assails my nostrils without warning, even though I was expecting it. Senem registers my unease, offers me a mask, which I accept gladly.

"I no longer smell it," she says, apologizing. "But I know

it's there. I wash my things every day. I'm frightened in case it won't come off."

The already-prepared coffins are stacked up against the walls, two rows and three deep on the sides of the hangar. By the door, bodies wait on metal trays laid out on the trolleys, five trays to a trolley. On the ground, there are a few more bodies, just bones, laid out on brown paper. The atmosphere is different from the last time, as if, with the dead now having been identified as people, the space has transformed into a place of grief. Maybe it is the green shrouds that cover the coffins that evoke the funerary images for me.

"For ten days we have been preparing the bodies," Senem says. "It's taken longer this year."

Of the 284 bodies to be buried on Sunday, 256 come from Tomašića. In total, 395 bodies have been identified thanks to Senem and her team's work. Not all will be interred this year, because some families have made a different decision for now. A lot of the relatives need more time to organize themselves or bring relatives together, the children and cousins scattered across the globe, from Australia to the United States.

The smell is difficult for me to bear, despite the mask. Senem realizes this, suggests that we go outside. We sit down on the two benches opposite the entrance, I remember the color of the tiles on the ground. Brown and beige. The poster above the door is the same as it was four years ago: the little girl with dark eyes, standing amidst anonymous tombs marked with just NN[1], hands clutching a photo of her father, above, the phrase: *where is my father?*

"It was hard finding a solution for the bodies, Senem tells me. "At first, I put in a quote for refrigerated containers. It was far too expensive and added to that, we would have had to buy a new generator to supply them all. Then, I put in one to refriger-

---

1 No-Name

ate a third of the hangar. But that would have needed important building works, costing several thousand euros, to lower the ceiling, isolate it all, and even with all this, we wouldn't have managed to get below sixteen degrees. Because to conserve bodies, it must be between five and twelve degrees. Impossible. And let's not even talk about the cost of three months of electricity with either of those setups!"

They had, in fact, promised her money, but Senem never saw any of it. As a result, she went looking herself. She thought to herself that there must be a solution. One thing was for sure: the bodies could not be left in this state. "Can you imagine what it was like here when the bodies started to decompose. Very quickly, we had fungi, insects, larvae. When we would open a body bag, it would be swarming. It was not possible, not for the victims, the families, or us. We had to do something. And so, I asked myself the question what did people do, before, to keep bodies, meaning when you didn't have cold rooms or electricity? That is what made me think of mummies. I read everything I could on the subject, and I came upon the idea of salt. They used to use that, the Egyptians: salt. It had never been tested out in mortuary anthropology, so I tried it. And it worked."

Senem invented her own method of mummification, inspired by the Egyptian one. First a layer of salt on the tray, then a layer of gauze, so that the salt would not directly attack the body. Then a second layer placed on the remains, before a covering of another layer of salt. The salt absorbs the liquids, dries out the body and halts the decomposition. "Creatures cannot live in salt," Senem explains. "And we checked: salt does not alter DNA."

I listen, fascinated. I remember Senem at the bar at the Hotel Le Pont ten months earlier, thinking aloud, with no solution to keep the bodies in some kind of dignified state. What kind of tenacity is she capable of to search out a way in the history books, bearing in mind this is why we have electricity, and all this boils down, ultimately, to an issue of money?

When the prosecutor gave her authorization to use salt on all the bodies, Senem ordered several tons. With the gauze, in total and for everything, it cost 1500 in convertible marks (KM), or 750 in euros. She says that she is proud of her discovery because it can work elsewhere, "In poor countries like our own," after earthquakes or other natural disasters, when you have to manage large numbers of victims and keep their bodies for the time it takes for identification.

"The day I put the gauze and the salt on all the bodies, I had the sense that I was finally restoring their dignity to them."

That day also marked the three-month point in her wait for the hypothetical cold-room that would never come. Three months of work in a hangar with the stench of death, without a solution, during an exceptionally clement winter. "Right, I have to go back in," Senem says, "Zlatan is waiting for me." I follow her, I feel better, the smell has become tolerable. In the end, I stayed five hours in the morgue, watching Senem and Zlatan repeat the same procedure over and over again.

One trolley after another, they work through them. From each, they remove the five trays that the trolley holds, and place them on the ground. They lift off the gauze with its layer of encrusted salt covering the body, roll it up by the side of the tray. Afterwards, they get hold of the other layer of gauze underneath and lift up the mummified body, place it on a clean bodybag, inside which they will also put the carefully folded up old body-bag, the one still bearing the code written in black felt tip, with the inscription TO for Tomašića.

Under the awning, where Zlatan usually washes the bodies, a table has been set up. This is where the placing in the coffins occurs, in lightweight ones made up of a simple wooden frame on which a green cloth is hung. Two male volunteers from the Muslim community are in charge of the whole task, doing it like an assembly line. First, they get hold of the plank which will serve as the bottom of the coffin, then on it, they place the body bag and personal effects. Afterwards they attach the curved ribs that will give the coffin its rounded shape and on which they will hang the green shroud bordered with a gold fringe, which is stapled to the plank. Clunk-clunk, clunk-clunk. The sound of the staple-gun reverberates instead of the usual sound of the Kärcher that I am accustomed to. To finish off, a final clunk-clunk affixes a plastic sleeve containing a sheet of paper indicating the surname, name, name of the father, date of birth and the date and place of death. I think back to the mass grave, to the sheet inserted into a plastic sleeve and photographed next to a body newly risen from the soil, indicating the date and place of its exhumation.

Between these two sheets of paper, exists the work of Senem and her team.

Upright against the hangar wall, other planks are propped, more of the curved ribs, a saw, a hammer. The coffins are the same for all, except one, which resembles the coffins that I recognize: a wooden box, with a cross. It is the coffin of a Croat Catholic.

Standing between the trolleys, Senem smokes one of her slender cigarettes. She does not always have the time to finish them before she must get back to work, in which case she keeps the lit cigarette in the corner of her mouth and grabs hold of another tray. The salt, the gauze, the body-bag, salt, gauze, body-bag. The empty trays are piled up in a corner, the salt thrown to the ground, sometimes it needs be broken up because it is so encrusted. Senem takes a pickaxe to break up the salt crust from the bottom of a tray, the salt comes away in plaques that shatter on the ground, white heaps which she picks up with a large blue shovel, a snow shovel. Sometimes, the empty trays are too heavy for Senem, Zlatan takes over. "It is because of my fall in the mass grave last October, my elbow and arm still hurt a bit," she says, apologizing.

"Come over," she calls to me from the other side of the hangar, where, once the placing in coffins is completed, the coffins are arranged by village and by family, and by the cemetery to which they will eventually be taken. Senem points out a pile. "You know Mirsad, don't you? That's his family. His grandmother, his grandfather, his father, his brother, his uncle and two cousins. Three generations. His brother was only fifteen years old.

I know Mirsad's story. I remember Sudbin, at the edge of the mass grave, telling me: "Can you imagine the hope this place represents for him?" I feel the tears rising up. Losing that amount of people that you love, is insane, as if the sheer number means each individual life gets drowned out, when really each fate is different, each death unique. How can one, simultaneously, grieve one's grandparents, father and adolescent brother, when their deaths taken on their own are already terrible? I try to make sense of the names on the sheets, all these Duratovićs, an entire family in front of me.

"Have you ever discussed any of this with the Serbs? They have the missing on their side too," Senem asks me, lighting a cigarette.

I have the feeling that she is reading my thoughts. I have been asking myself this question for a while: What memory of the war remains on the side of those, who, in the eyes of the world, have found themselves in the role of the persecutor, whether they chose it or not? "That is what I want to do now," I answer. "But it will take me time. And then again, I'm not exactly sure what it is I'm looking for."

"You are just looking for answers to your questions."

"I imagine so, yes. The closer I get to this story, the more I feel like it is beyond my reach. The more it seems impossible to tackle. And sometimes, I ask myself what I am getting myself into, in spite of myself. What am I taking part in. I do not feel like I have a grasp of all the issues, they elude me."

"I understand. Personally, I think I'm going to boycott the funerals. I'm sick of politicians who come to be in the public eye, to give lofty speeches. They come because it is election time soon, and they come as if they are campaigning. Where does it get us when they do this? For me, the only thing that counts in the face of this tragedy, is to be silent. To read out the names of the deceased, and that is it. Nothing more. "

Senem seems annoyed. I recognize the flash of irritation when she talks about the politicians, the ones who object to the release of the funds that would allow her to do the job properly, the ones who hold forth about the war in front of the TV cameras but are never anywhere to be found when it comes to buying the refrigerated containers that would stop the larvae eating the dead bodies.

"Where were they, all these people, when we needed a solution here? Where were they this winter when one day we had no electricity, no internet or telephone, because the bills had not been paid? Where were they to pay for the cold-rooms when we know they had enough funds in their bank accounts for several? On top of it, this year, apparently there is a VIP zone at the funerals, for foreign dignitaries and politicians, so they won't be too hot. We can't have them being too hot, this lot, while the families will be out there under the scorching heat." She has raised her voice without realizing it, her voice choked with anger.

"No, I won't go on Sunday, I will come here on Saturday morning, to say goodbye to the bodies when the trucks come for them. I know I've done everything that had to be done for the deceased, for their families, and that is all that matters."

From under the awning, the clunk-clunk of the nail-gun can be heard. The stacks are getting ever higher. "All of this is a disgrace" says Senem and gestures with her whole arm towards the expanse of the hangar, the wall with photographs of the missing, the bodies still laid out on the ground. She repeats: "This for me, here, is a disgrace. This place needs to be different, with an area to receive people, giving them the space to reflect and gather themselves, to find out information. But there is nothing."

She stubs out her cigarette, goes back to work. Salt, gauze, body-bag. Move the tray. Break the salt. Next tray. It is hot, she sponges her sweat-covered forehead. The sound of the staple-gun puncturing the wood of the coffins gives a rhythm to their movements. Standing alone in the corner, I watch, as they work in silence, the exhaustion of the day beginning to show. I no longer need a mask. Clunk clunk. A green shroud stretched at each end, clunk-clunk, on the sides, clunk clunk-clunk-clunk.

"Last day tomorrow!" pipes up one of the men who is busy with the placing in coffins. What does he think of my presence, my observing gaze? I could not say whether it is annoyance or fatigue. Sometimes, I sense him observing me back.

Around 4PM, Senem stops, her face dripping with sweat. The day is done. Still waiting on the trays, the last 25 bodies will have to be left for tomorrow.

"Exhausted?"

"Oh, you know, to be honest, I prefer physical exhaustion to mental fatigue. This winter, there were moments when it just got too much, between here and the NN project, I had to be everywhere all at once."

For nearly a year, as well as running the Šejkovača morgue, Senem has been coordinating a team that reviews all the non-identified cases—The NN cases—across all the country's morgues. A sort of review of the cold cases that have waited for sometimes up to twenty years without a match to a living person's DNA. The body-bags must be re-opened, the documentation retrieved—photos, exhumation reports and the autopsy —and sometimes new DNA tests undertaken. Three thousand cases of this type exist.

The project turned out to be more complicated than expected. In a country forced to split in two by the war, into the Serb Republic of Bosnia and the Federation of Bosnia-Herzegovina, the number of missing is also a political issue. The numbers can be brandished as weapons to incite rancor and stoke fears. And since a "case" can refer to something as simple as a femur bone as it can a whole body, the numbers are easy to manipulate. After just a few weeks, Senem and her team realized that many of the cases had nothing to do with the 1992-1995 war. Some dated back to the Second World War, others had no link whatsoever to any particular conflict.

"I travel all over Bosnia with this project," says Senem, lighting the last smoke of the day. "I go to spots I do not know very well. As an example, we worked in the Mostar cemetery. It is so beautiful, the most beautiful cemetery in the country. One day, during the break, I went off to walk along some of its rows and I noticed a particularly beautiful tomb, the tomb of a young woman, Marsela Sunjic. I asked my colleagues if they knew about her. They explained to me she was a writer from Mostar who published two books. I bought and read them. Have you ever heard of her?"

"No, never."

"Taina, I could not even read one book about the war before, not a single account. I live with the consequences of war every day. Marsela Šunjić's books only talk about this, the war. So, for the first time, I read one and it was so accurate. This is what it was like, the war. I researched her, I saw her books had been translated into several languages, but here, in Bosnia, the country that Marsela talks about, no one knows her. Do you see how much we are blind?"

She drags on her cigarette, looks at the rows of coffins, this, her everyday job, a job born out of the war while she was dreaming of being an archaeologist.

"With this project, I see how each person tells their own truth about this story. Increasingly, I ask what it means for us, as a nation. How is it possible that in certain regions of this country, Srebrenica is a genocide but in others, it is not? How is it possible that when you get to Banja Luka, Srebrenica no longer exists." I just listen, I don't have an answer. I don't know if it's even possible, twenty years after the war, to agree on one version of the truth at the level of a nation. It is certainly possible to see events from the perspective of a person, a situation, and to see the nuances, the context—for example, Sudbin's father's former colleague, who saved Sudbin's and his brother's life, while also being part of a death squad—but to establish the truth at this national level, I don't know how that is done. I think of the few hours I spent at the Radovan Karadžić trial at the International Criminal Tribunal for the Former Yugoslavia, in the Hague. The accused, put on trial for genocide and crimes against humanity, gave as an explanation for one of the many mass graves in Srebrenica, that one of the victims had been buried for 'for hygiene purposes,' and not to hide a crime. His daughter, Sonja Karadžić-Jovičević, had just put herself forward as an MP for the Serb Republic of Bosnia in the parliamentary elections. Rows of coffins stand in front of me, with seven people from the same family, what shared truth can be constructed from this? In the end, to forge a nation, maybe it's better to hope for qualification in a major football championship rather than a shared interpretation of history.

When she drops me at the bus station, Senem talks to me again about her desire to do something different, her farm project, the medicinal plants.

"I feel rootless," she says. "I need to settle down, to return to the land of my ancestors, to say to myself they were here."

Then she adds:

"I want to be happy."

"You want to grow living things."

"You could put it like that as well."

6

YOU MUST CHERISH WHAT MAKES LIFE SWEET

I t is my third night spent alone in the house and I know now that at 7:30AM, a chill will still be in the air, but one hour later, the sun will already be beating down so intensely that it will be impossible for me to stay on the terrace, the glare too much for my eyes, and the sun will burn my face. The dog belonging to Mehmed's sister-in-law, Nina, comes to say hello, he's been prowling around the surrounding area ever since his mistress left for a retirement home, leaving the little detached house next-door empty. Yesterday, while I spent the day in the house and garden, the animal kept me company, sleeping on the gravel while I took a siesta upstairs to escape the heat.

When I woke up, the sky had darkened, and thunder rumbled in the distance. I sat on the terrace to watch the clouds traverse the sky, listen to the wind whip up and surge through the leaves of the apple and linden trees in the garden, a kind of music that starts gently but slowly gets louder, rustling in each branch, each leaf, before departing. The thunder got closer, the storm erupted. Large droplets of water drummed the metal lid of the well, and my legs stretched out in the rain, a cold rain that dispelled the heavy hours of sun and heat.

I remained like that, listening to the thunder and the rain, and something fell into place within me after a tormented spring, the sorrow of an ending in my life. Something in me found peace.

I had decided to go and see Rasma in the morning. I find her in her vegetable garden, busying herself behind the house. She stops to sit down with me on the terrace, is so insistent about offering me a coffee that I relent, even though it is Ramadan and I know she is fasting. She serves me a Bosnian coffee, my first Bosnian coffee of this stay, thick and strong. We speak in German, our only language in common, which I make a mess of and which Rasma masters perfectly because of her years spent in Germany. I show her pictures of my children, I want to share a little bit of my life with her, let her see who I am when I am at home with my nearest and dearest. With Rasma, we got to know each other in that very particular way that you do when you are a journalist, by asking them to share the story of their lives, their innermost self, without revealing too much of your own.

Sitting on the terrace, a cup of steaming coffee in front of me, I listen to Rasma tell me about the most recent news from the village. Yesterday, she was in Kozarac for an interview with investigators who had come from Sarajevo, a man and a woman who had come to question witnesses about events here during the war. They asked her questions for four hours.

"Four hours!" exclaims Rasma. And on top of that, it is Ramadan. I don't eat anything, I don't drink anything! At one point, they suggested I have a break, but I said: "What's the point of a break, I'm going to carry on thinking about it all anyway, so I might as well tell you it all in one go, to get it over with. So, I said everything I had to say, everything that I witnessed. What I hadn't seen, I couldn't talk about, but everything I saw, I said."

And she has seen things, Rasma. She had told me a part of it during my interview with her for the web documentary. As the village of Trnopolje was being emptied of its non-Serb inhabitants, either chased away or imprisoned in the school that was turned into a detention camp during the spring of 1992, Rasma decided to stay, spending the summer and autumn months in a house adjoining the camp. She rummaged in the abandoned houses to find what she could to cook food for the prisoners. The Serb soldiers did not stop her; perhaps this small round woman who had decided to do exactly as she pleased had made an impression on them.

Yesterday, the investigators came to pick her up by car, arriving at her house.

"Then I came home by taxi, I paid for it myself," she said.

"They could have paid for your taxi, at the very least."

She makes a gesture with her hand which seems to both mean "no point" and "don't hold your breath." Perhaps they had offered to drop her back in the car, but she had declined, preferring a taxi rather than coming back in a car which everyone would have noticed. It was enough that she had been seen leaving with them....

"You know Nina is in a retirement home? When she saw the images at Tomašića on the TV last autumn, it was too much for her. After that, all she wanted to do was pack her bags and leave."

" I saw her dog," I replied. He comes to the house.

"Yes, Rocky. She talks about him all the time. Her house

and her dog. Things are better for her now."

"And your son, will he come to stay in Bosnia this summer, with the kids?"

"Yes, next week! They are by the sea now, in Croatia. The twins are already six years old. Can you imagine! They will start school in the autumn." She gets out a photo, shows me the round faces of children.

"My older son has built a house a little further on, eight kilometers from here, the younger one as well. That way, they have a place for the holidays. Everyone is building such big houses, even though they only come for a few weeks a year. The neighbor over there, near Emira's home, he lives in Sweden and he built a house with eighteen rooms! Can you believe it! Eighteen rooms! What is the point? They are hardly ever here!" She makes a face, one of incomprehension to underline her point, to make sure that I understand despite my deficient German. Then she shrugs, gestures towards the terrace and garden. "As for me, I'm good here, in my little house, with my little garden. Before, I had a large house, a car, a motorcycle, a tractor, land, I had all that and in one week, it was gone. Nothing left. So, why bother to have all these things? Now, I have my little Barbie house, my garden, my vegetable patch, and it's just fine like this."

"And you, you are the little Barbie doll inside."

"A very round Barbie if I am!" she replies, bursting out laughing.

"But no Ken."

"Oh no, no Ken. That's all finished! '*And where are you going? And what are you doing?*' No, no, all that is done. I want to be free, that's it."

I ask her what she is growing in her vegetable garden this year. She finds my curiosity funny. "You're like Mirela, she as well, she always wants to know this kind of thing." Then she leads me behind the house, to her little green sanctuary in the back where she spends hours pampering her plants. "Look! there are potatoes, onions, eggplants, tomatoes, green beans, white beans, spinach, peppers of course, parsley, dill, turnips, cabbages, large and small cucumbers, they're better, the smaller ones. What shall I get you? Well, yes, of course I'm going give you some. You eat everything, don't you? Do you cook paprika pods? It's very simple, you do them in the frying pan, you add some cream, and five minutes later, they're ready and they're delicious. You must absolutely take some! No, that's not too much for you. You do eat paprika, right?"

I returned home with a bag full of vegetables. I stopped at the grocery store to buy some Kajmak, a locally made thick cream, slightly sour, and some cigarettes for Mehmed who was due to arrive that night with Emira and Mirela. I took a different way to get home, by the road this time, I looked at the rebuilt houses, the eighteen-room type, as if they were a way to thumb their noses at those who had destroyed everything: you think you crushed me—well, here you are, take a look at my house now, even bigger than before! Along the five kilometers that separate Trnopolie from Korazac, there are scores of houses like this, immense, with ornate balconies, elaborate columns, and imposing front gates. When you start heading up to the heights of Korazac, you get the impression that they are all trying to outdo the excess of each other. They fill up in the summer, when the Bosniak diaspora returns and multiplies the number of inhabitants in the surrounding villages by ten. In the autumn, they are shuttered up, the doors are locked, only the gardening companies' employees stay around— a new industry in the area over the last few years— they pass by to check the gardens now and then. Those who live here all year-round have the smallest houses, often in rough brick; they returned to their lives from before, but did not have the salaries of those who went abroad.

And then there are the ruins, sometimes just a concrete slab which the vegetation has begun to conceal, the weeds growing on the walls. Earlier, Rasma had pointed out the house opposite, a gutted red brick house, roofless, the door and window openings like gaping holes, left abandoned for years.

"It's sad," she had said to me. "Before the war, they had just built the house, then the war came and the Chetniks[2] took everything inside, even the electricity cables, everything! As for them now, they live in the United States, they only came back once, then never returned. Why don't they sell the land? Someone else could build a house. I don't know why they won't sell. It's a shame."

As I walk home, I wonder if it is impossible for them to let go of this last bond with a country that they were forced to flee. Whereas Rasma has watched life carry on— what else could she see, living here, each day, other than the necessity that life must continue?—perhaps this now-American family would feel like they were erasing the last vestiges of their origins by giving up the little that remains here. Or, maybe the business of selling when you are on the other side of the world is just too complicated. As for Rasma, she would prefer a reconstructed and occupied house opposite her own, rather than this constant reminder of the war.

At home, I cook my paprikas with red onions and with the Kajnak, I taste it, close my eyes, savouring the flavours of the place, I think of Rasma in her vegetable garden, the love and care that she devotes to her vegetables, and again I am reminded of Sudbin's words, the day that I arrived: "You must cherish what makes life sweet."

In the evening, the inhabitants of the house are back, a kiss hello for Emira and Mirela, cigarettes for Mehmed, our custom for the last four years since I have been coming over. I swap English and German for French, and we talk late into the night, sampling Emira's homemade cherry liqueur. She tells me

2. Used here to describe the Serb militias in the Balkan war, but originally Serb guerrilla units that fought in World War I and in World War II, armed bands of Serbs active in Yugoslavia during its occupation (1941–1945).

about her summer building projects, her last round of planting in the garden, the news from her winter spent with Mehmed in France. They have lived there since 1992, arriving as refugees with their two girls then aged ten and eight, knowing nothing about the country or the language, relieved to be alive, albeit bruised, by Mehmed's months in the camps and Emira's on the road, and eventually managing to escape the country with their two daughters.

Since then, the girls have grown up, Mirela has come back to Bosnia to live—in Tuzla—and Medina has made her life in France, while the parents go back and forth—the winter months spent over there, the summer ones back here—in this house that they have rebuilt.

"Mum was worrying about you," Mirela tells me, teasing. "She thought that you might be frightened here with all the stories that you now know about this place."

"You mustn't worry about me," I say with a smile to Emira, who looks a bit embarrassed. "I'm still very happy to be here in your home."

The next day, I wake up thinking of Senem. Today is the day that 284 coffins will leave Šejkovača. She will be overseeing their loading onto the trucks, watching on as they depart, these bodies that she brought out of the earth; seeing them leave the hangar where they have spent the last ten months waiting, beneath the salt that she discovered in the history books.

The trucks will drive the forty-five kilometers from the morgue to Korazac village, they will pass through Prijedor, cross the town, take the road for Banja Luka, then turn right at the big junction, where the road forks between Korazac and Trnopolje. They will stop in front of Korazac stadium before being unloaded, and the coffins will be lined up on the turf the full length of the football field, for the all-night vigil and the ceremony of the next day.

Three days ago, when I was in Šejkovača, Senem spoke to

me again about the smell. "I don't know how it will be. It risks being very hot. With the body-bags and the shroud, it should reduce it a bit, but I think there will be an odor all the same." The idea made her uncomfortable, for the families. And a little for the dead as well. She would have preferred that they be buried without being exposed to the sun, wind and night-time humidity.

After breakfast, I send her a text: "Dear Senem, I am thinking of you this morning. Your work restoring the dignity to the dead is precious."

She answers me a little later in the day: "It was a very emotionally charged day for me. Thank you for your support."

In the evening, sitting in the bus station bar in Prijedor, I wait for Mirela. The last bus calling at the junction of Trnopolje and Kozarac has left already, and she has promised to come by and get me by car. I settle down on the terrace of the Buffet Time Out, one of those anonymous bars devoid of any charm, serving passing travellers, any fashionable décor or sophisticated menu being pointless. The only other client is a bald man of a certain age, leaning on his cane with one hand and stroking his salt and pepper moustache with the other. The seats with red cushions advertize Nektar beer, its round tables are covered in blue plastic tablecloths, decorated with little rows of flowers of yellow and pale mauve. Young girls in t-shirts and little shorts are crossing the road pulling their suitcases behind them. It is summer in Prijedor.

Earlier, I had seen Nemanja in a café on the other side of the river. A coke for me, a beer for him. At the end, he apologized: "I am totally broke. I don't have a penny." He is still struggling to find work, still dreams of leaving Bosnia. He looks both dubious and amused when I tell him that I have come for the holidays, and for the funerals. "A holiday? Here, in this country, in this town?" I must seem totally crazy to him, he who dreams of another life far removed from this horizonless place.

I tell him about my desire to return, to tell another part of the story, the "memory war" still playing out. I do not really know what he thinks about it. He talks to me about the few memories that he still has of the war, childhood memories, a little hazy or conversely, incredibly sharp, such as his mother's words when they had to take refuge in a cave: "Anything can happen now. They're taking Prijedor right at this moment." He was seven or eight years old, his father was on the front, while he was in a cave with his mother and little sister. Shortly afterwards, they left the town and took refuge with an uncle, or a cousin— he no longer remembers—around the Koraza Mountain, away from the fighting. Then his mother sent him with his brother to Serbia, to her family village.

"During the tradition of Slava, when a family's patron saint is celebrated, you must recount the story of war," he explains to me.

"For example, like what?" I ask.

"You don't want to know. I promise, you really don't want to know."

"Why?

"Because... I think people have become contaminated with all the political problems of this country, all the stories they hear. In my case, what I do in those moments, is, I stay quiet. In my family, I am always the one who disagrees with others' views, I don't want to spend my whole time arguing."

The sun is beginning to set behind the buildings around the station, the heat of the afternoon is lifting. All that remains is the balminess of the day ending, a gentle feel on my arms, for just a few moments more before the coolness of night comes, and the the shivering begins.

Nemanja is right. It is probably a strange idea to come and spend your holidays here, in this country, this town, for this occasion, surrounded by these stories. And yet, the place heals me and I feel in the right place, that of a stranger who writes in her notebook on the terrace of the Buffet Time Out, while the suns sets and just one old man with his cane keeps me company at the round tables, with the blue tablecloths dotted with rows of yellow and pale mauve flowers. No, lilac. That is it, the word that I was looking for. The yellow and lilac flowers.

In the car as we head to Korazac, Mirela tells me about her visit to the retirement home to see her aunt Nina, earlier in the day. When the trucks loaded with coffins were about to pass just in front of the building, situated on the road between Prijedor and Banja Luka, she led Nina inside so that she would not see the cortège.

"I hope that tomorrow, somebody will be there to keep her occupied, to talk about something else. I hope that over there, none of this exists, either today or tomorrow," she says, driving us to the vigil. "She doesn't want to bury her son for now. She wants to wait, you never know, perhaps they will find a bit more if there are other excavations. But when it does go ahead, like so many of the mothers..." Mirela hesitates before finishing her sentence. "I don't know how she'll survive that moment."

In Korazac, the stadium's environs are already plunged in darkness. Inside, the floodlights illuminate the football field. The coffins are set out on the green turf, side by side, the whole length of the field. Relatives have set up beside them, some have brought carpets to sit on the grass, others wander between the coffins, looking for a familiar name, kneel to place a hand on the green shroud and say a prayer. A lot have come as family groups, the children clutching a father's or a grandmother's hand. In front of one of the coffins, a man has installed a plastic chair, sat down in it, motionless, in the halo of a stadium spotlight. Later on, he removes the chair and kneels in the same spot to pray or simply be a little closer to the person to whom he is saying goodbye.

The next day the stadium is jam-packed. So many people are there, I do not even attempt to go in. Mirela neither. Her parents and Rasma have seated themselves to the side of the stadium, in the shade of some trees, Emira has got out a little fold-able stool for Mehmed. I stay apart. I need solitude and silence. I walk between the trucks, the trailers and the vans parked on the road's curb, all along the stadium fence on the other side of which the coffins are lined up, between the platform erected for the speeches and prayers, and the cramped rows of all those who have come to engage in private prayer, the men in front, the women behind.

Gathered in front of the platform, photographers, TV cameras, journalists with mics in hand, await the arriving pol-iticians and officials dressed in dark suits, flanked by body-guards and the policeman who will ensure order. Faced with this crowd, I understand that I have definitively abandoned my journalist's eye.

I slip in and out of the shade of the trucks, where it reeks of gas and brakes and flowers have been fastened to their pan-els, slid into the eyelets of their tarpaulins, even taped to the canvas. Roses, Sweet William, dandelions, wilted already by the sun blazing down on the village today.

The trucks are always featured in this story, they are pres-ent at every stage, in Čarakovo, Zecovi, Hambarine, Tomašića and Jakarina Kosa. Some of the men here today, standing in the packed rows, have memories and images of such trucks load-ed with bodies leaving the Keraterm camp, bloodstains on the tarmac. Maybe in a genocide, the first people to be interviewed should be the truck-drivers, the drivers of the buses and trains. They are the ones who know. Like the chauffeur who led the investigators to the mass grave at Tomašića.

Today, the trucks total fourteen, spanning the length of the stadium, their back doors open. Some are decorated with Bosnia-Herzegovina flags. The dead that they will transport lat-er on to the cemeteries did not know that this country would exist one day, with this flag, with this national anthem that they have just sung in the stadium. The thought makes me sad. Their death still makes no sense at all, even if they had known. They died because of madness, because of hatred and fear incited to serve power. Here, they are called martyrs, as if to endow, *a posteriori*, their death with meaning.

After the speeches and prayers, the coffins, carried by relatives, friends, acquaintances, depart the stadium, towards the trucks, whose cargo-bays swallow them up. I watch the coffins advance, hands holding them aloft at shoulder level. Dozens and dozens of green shrouds file in front of my eyes, as the names of the deceased are read over the microphone. I listen to the long list of the Duratovićs, who are Mirsad's family. I see him from afar, talking with the drivers. He might have just buried seven members of his family today, but he is also part of an organization. He has lost weight, his face is worn out, he looks fifty although he is, like me, forty. He is directing with his hands, which truck goes first, whether a police car is required between two particular trucks, no, it will be OK, and he jumps into his car and gets going in turn.

It is hot. I feel the sweat streaming down my back, along my covered arms, beneath my scarf, and I think of the families out there, under the sun, for hours, many of whom have been there since the evening before, having spent the night on the site, keeping vigil over the bodies and fasting during Ramadan.

Yesterday, I reread the list: I could not find the names of Fikret's children and wife.

I watch as the trucks go off, a funerary cortège of articulated trailers and vans, windows open because of the smell, almost imperceptible in the open air, but concentrated in the vehicle cabins. It immediately prompts images for me of the mass grave, the morgue and the salt-covered bodies.

I think about Senem again who had watched the same cortège yesterday when the bodies left Šejkovaća. How did she say goodbye to them, all these dead that pass through her hands? I want to tell her not to worry, the odor is okay, you did everything that needed to be done.

Although I watch the trucks set off for the surrounding cemeteries, I decide not to follow them. My story with these dead comes to a close at this point. This thought arrives peacefully to me. I walk up the road, cross the already empty stadium, where the speakers are being packed up, the platform dismantled. Not one trace of the bodies or the ceremony remain on the green turf, save a few empty water bottles.

I walk up the main street, to my usual café, I order a lemonade. The holiday makers wander on the *čaršija*, the main artery through the village and a meeting point for people, where you come across acquaintances, chat about the news of the last year. Little by little, the empty terraces fill up again, coffees are ordered, a chat with a cousin come from Germany, another from the United States who has not been seen for several years. The cars parked along the length of the pavement display number plates from the four corners of Europe, from Sweden to Italy. The music was silent for the day of mourning, but already a poster on a tree announces an event for the next day, a concert at the Stara Bašta restaurant, and for the weekend after, another hosted by the aquatic park next to the Grand Mosque.

In the evening, in the Maroslićs' garden, the iftar meal lingers into the night, but it is not the usual atmosphere of the long dinners that break the fast, usually of hysterical laughter, chattering and shared confidences. Tonight, the past looms continuously, everyone is suddenly hypersensitive. Between words and silence, the hesitation of whether to talk about it or something else to avoid the subject is a constant presence. In the end the choice makes no difference, the air remains heavy with memories, with pain and with an absence that can never be filled. It is suffocating.

During the night, their stories intrude into my dreams. I dream of my son in a camp, my father in a camp, finding comfort in the idea that that they are there together, but pierced by the guilt of not having managed to stop what has happened.

When I wake up, I am fuzzy-headed. Mehmed is already

waiting for me in the kitchen, I make some coffee for us both and he decides that we will drink it out on the terrace. We get comfortable, with our cups and cafetiere, and we drink our coffee. He revises his French with me and I my Bosnian with him, then we fall into silence. I am comfortable with him. A cow lows in the distance. "Krava," Mehmed tells me, and I repeat: "krava". Then I say "vache," and he replies: "Yes, cow." Then he gets up to smoke a cigarette, I take the cups back to the kitchen, sit on one of the beige sofas as the sun slips through the curtain panels on the door, wedged open by a pair of fuchsia pink and apple green slippers. Right by them, atop a pale wood stool, on a lace doily, a radio plays an Elvis song and Mehmed's helmet is set against the backrest of the sofa opposite. I want to remember this image, the slippers, the lace mat, the helmet and the oblique light of the morning. This story is no longer just a story, but the lived experience of my friends, their memories, their nightmares, their lives, of which an infinitesimal part now lives with me.

7

I LIKE TREES

arija has brought me to the terrace of the Hotel Vrbas, a wooden terrace on stilts over the river of the same name. She has chosen a table in the corner, in the cool shade of a huge and beautiful tree of which there are many in Banja Luka. The city was never bombarded during the war, hence the trees survived. Darija has eyes the color of aqua and a gaze that pierces you, the gaze of someone who knows a thing or two about human stories.

"I like trees," she says rolling a cigarette," especially this one."

She has a husky voice and blond hair pulled into a chignon atop her head, a few rebel strands falling at her nape, and is wearing white jeans and a navy-blue t-shirt.

Darija is a friend of Senem's. She works for the ICMP as well, in the blood collection department. She travels to visit with the relatives of the missing, to gather ante-mortem information from them, and then take their blood samples that will allow, through DNA comparison, the identification of the bodies recovered from the mass graves. She is the one who re-assured Senem when she'd burst into tears at the sight of a run-over cat on the road to Banja Luka, who told her that she too can find herself losing it over the tiniest thing. "Go see Darija," Senem had said to me, a few days earlier in the pause between two bodies being laid to rest in their coffin at Šejkovača. "Now she, she is a Serb, go see Darija".

And so that morning, I took a train to the little station of Trnopolje, in one of those old trains that still have nicely padded seats and equally stuffed ashtrays and are beginning a second life in Bosnia. This one was made in Sweden, I recognized the word *avfallskorg* above the litter bin. The carriage smelt of stale tobacco, my ticket had been handwritten by the sole employee of the station, reminding me of my adolescence in Finland, my country of birth only discovered at age fifteen when I had roamed across it by train, drunk on that new-found freedom of being allowed to travel on my own.

Darija was waiting for me at Banja Luka station and had brought me here, under this giant tree. She finishes rolling her cigarette, lights it, stirs her newly arrived coffee and asks me: "So, what is it you are looking for?"

I am caught short by the question. I reply with the only thing that seems absolutely certain to me at this particular moment. "I think I am looking for a reason to come back here."

This makes her smile.

"I am trying to understand how it was here, for those who did not need to leave," I add.

"I see."

" How long have you been working for the ICMP?"

"I began in 2000, one year before Senem. That is how we met. "

She continues to stir her coffee, takes a drag on her cigarette and starts to tell the story. "It happened by chance. The war had already ended for five years, I was doing little jobs here and there. I had wanted to study art but the war had passed through this area and my parents did not have the means to fund me. It was my brother who saw the ad. He was a chauffeur for the office of the High Representative[3] at the time. The ICMP was looking for people for the blood collections department. I thought to myself why not. It was only meant to be a one-year contract. This year it will be fifteen years!," she says laughing.

In the beginning, Darija only met with Serb families. The tension between the two communities was such that it was difficult to do it any other way. The Banja Luka office had been opened precisely for this reason, so teams coming from Tuzla, a town on the Federation of Bosnia-Herzegovina side, would not have to go to the Serb Republic of Bosnia side where they would not have been well received. Darija, who is Serb by her father and Croat by her mother, and from the town of Banja Luka, worked with five other colleagues. There was also an office in Sanski Most whose population was predominantly made up of Bosniak refugees. Its premises were located by the bus station, where I had gotten off the bus arriving for the first time at the Šejkovaća morgue.

Then, as requirement decreased, that particular office was closed, and the decision was made to retain only one investigator in Banja Luka—that being Darija. This is how she found herself in charge, by herself, of a third of the country which she travels across by car, from village to village, gathering information on missing people and taking blood samples from relatives.

3. The High Representative, is the supreme politician of the region, appointed by the European Union. A post-war measure still in place, and which effectively makes Bosnia- Herzegovina a protectorate of the European Union. (All notes are from the author.

"I live in my car," she says, smiling. It is a small blue car, with diplomatic number plates, due to the diplomatic status of the ICMP. Now I am the one to smile at this little detail. Neither Darija nor her car fit the image of a diplomatic corp. She looks more like a kind of Balkan cowboy in her dented vehicle, roaming the roads, cigarette at the corner of her mouth.

She is not in complete agreement with her higher-ups' insistence that the need for investigators is decreasing. Over the last few years, a review of the official missing lists has not been enough for her, she likes to investigate directly. By dint of always working this way, ever-present on the ground, she is able to make an inventory of the missing unaccounted for in the records, the ones that nobody ever reported.

"To give an example, next to Banja Luka, there was a village that was completely destroyed. There is nothing left. The database does not even mention any of the missing people originally from this area—whereas necessarily, there must be! I went there in search of them and I eventually came across somebody who said all the people had fled to Croatia. The person gave me the name of a Croatian village. When I arrived home, I took the telephone book and I started to make calls. And there were indeed some missing, although no one had reported them. I contacted the Croatian authorities who authorized me to go and collect blood samples. No one has ever been interested in these families."

I can hear anger in Darija's voice, the same anger as in Senem's when she feels there has been a lack of respect towards the families or the dead.

"I believe everyone has the right to be heard, to be given full attention," Darija says, stubbing out her cigarette. "Sometimes, it takes five minutes, sometimes it lasts two hours. I go to them and I listen. Each time, I am touched by their stories, by their gestures. Often, the people have made preparations for my visit, they've gone looking for a photo if they have one. They have prepared coffee, cakes, they want me to stay for dinner or lunch."

"Have you ever been badly received by Bosniaks?"

"No, never. Of course, the Muslim families immediately know that I am Serb, because of my first name. But I have never felt rejection. Those who have lost someone are beyond hate."

"You think so?"

I tell her about two young adults that I had met, a brother and sister of around twenty years old, whom I came across in Čarakovo, in Sudbin's village. Their father had been killed during the July 1992 massacres, when they were three and five years old. Since then, they had lived in the United States with their mother. They were returning to Bosnia for the first time, to see the abandoned family home, to discover a country of which they had very few memories. Their words were full of hate:

'I will never set foot in Banja Luka,' the young American woman had said. 'If I had a Serb in front of me, I think I would want to kill him.' The sister didn't know that in front of her, was, as it happened, a Serb: Zoran, the interpreter present to accompany her and who had listened to her, in silence. He only allowed his anger to explode later, once in the car. 'What does she know, her? She comes here for two weeks, just to throw her anger in our face!'" Darija listens to my story, finishing up her coffee.

"Yes, but how old were they when they left, those two?" she shoots back. "They were tiny. All they have heard ever since are the stories told by the family in the United States. They have never heard anything else, so how do you expect them to think differently?" She has a point, I think to myself.

"Even here, the young only hear one version of the story. All those who were born after the war have grown up in a divided country. Even at school, they are taught different versions of history. For the Muslims, it is they who are the heroes. For the Serbs, it is the Serbs and for the Croats, it is the Croats. Nobody wants to be the vanquished in this war. And the young absorb this. I am stunned when I listen to them. It is like a sickness. They are contaminated. I'm not sure if I would want to raise children in this country. If it continues like this, in ten or fifteen years, we will have a new war."

She says this very calmly, like an assessment, as she rolls another cigarette and orders another coffee. Her words send a chill up my spine. I want to protest, to say no, surely not, then I think about what Švabo recounted after his visit to Dachau, to the site of the concentration camp. His reaction, when confronted with the memorial proclaiming—in numerous languages—"Never Again" had been this: 'It's nonsense,' Švabo had retorted. 'Fifty years after Dachau, I was in a camp too. They would have been better off writing: Shit happens.'

And so, I say nothing and order another café.

"I have understood a lot of things, thanks to my work," Darija says. "I meet a lot of people, I listen to their stories. But during the war, in Banja Luka, we had no idea what was happening in Kozarac, in Prijedor or in Trnopolje. Not a thing. It was a well-kept secret. I only learnt years after the war."

"Even so, it is strange," I protest. "The images that were circulated around the world, for example, those images of prisoners at Trnopolje, behind barbed wire. They were everywhere, on the TV, in the newspapers, from 1992."

"Yes, you had TV and the newspapers. Whereas we, we had no electricity, and the only news we got was from the front. We just had propaganda."

"How was it, Banja Luka, during the war?" I ask, though avoiding the stupid and improper question, "What was the war like?" that I dare not put into words.

"The place was full of people. The non-Serb population had been progressively driven out, but there were Serb refugees, turning up from everywhere. The streets were full, people were arriving any way possible, by car, by bike, on foot. In my neighborhood, we had a lot of Muslims. It is one of the oldest neighborhoods of Banja Luka, with families living there since time immemorial. And you know, here, one's neighbors are sometimes more important than one's family. During much of the war, our Muslim neighbors remained in their homes. They did not want to leave, and my father tried to protect them. When we knew the soldiers were going to come looking for non-Serbs, the neighbors came to our home to hide in our cellar. The soldiers banged on the door and we told them we were Serbs and there was nobody in our house. From 1995, it was no longer possible for that, it became too dangerous. The neighbors had to leave, all of them. But what makes me happy is that they came back. Our neighborhood is as it was before." I had never heard this kind of testimony until now. Darija tells me about the story of her brother, who was eighteen, the age for military service. He had decided that he would not take up arms. His parents suggested that he leave Bosnia. But, he refused to flee.

"For me as well, my parents wanted me to leave. They wanted to save their skin and protect their children. But I did not want to leave Banja Luka. What was I going to do somewhere else? All my friends were here."

Darija was thirteen years old then, my daughter's age. The age when we have no wish whatsoever to leave our friends, war or no war.

"And your brother?"

"He hid in the cellar, for four years, with two of his friends who did not want to leave either."

I hear the lapping of the river under the terrace, a man fishes on the opposite bank. I wonder what it must feel like to come out of a cellar after four years.

"Now, I wonder if I made the biggest mistake of my life, not leaving," Darija says suddenly.

"Seriously?"

"No, I'm joking... I don't really think that. But sometimes, when I look at the opportunities that opened up for those who left, yes, I do regret it. Of course, I have a job, I make a living, and I sincerely believe one can live well in Bosnia, even if the salaries are nothing like what you can earn abroad. But well... sometimes I can feel regret about it."

"And your brother?"

"It's alright. He is married now, he has a little girl of five. But living all that time with fear, it leaves a scar."

We have finished our coffees, Darija offers to show me her office. We cross the bridge overlooking the Vrbas River, then the town center with its shops. The ICMP premises is situated in a hospital building, above the forensic medicine department and the blood transfusion center. It occupies a whole floor, but the majority of its offices are now empty. Only Darija's and that of the director of the DNA laboratory remain, with his office at the other end of the corridor. The laboratory employs three people, along with the director. In it, they prepare bone samples, cleaning them, then crushing them to transform them into the dust that will allow for DNA extraction. The little drops of blood collected by Darija as samples are dealt with by another laboratory, in Tuzla, in the center of the country. Each year, the ICMP handles thousands of samples, which arrive into Bosnia-Herzegovina from all around the world, from Kosovo, from Iraq—everywhere in fact where the organization undertakes identification activities.

Darija's office is spartan, a large table with a computer, piles of paper, a shelf, a little fridge to store the blood samples before their dispatch to the laboratory. When she is not on the ground, she is here, inputting the gathered information to the databases, making phone calls, searching on the internet for the relatives of the missing. With time, this becomes increasingly difficult. People pass away, move or go abroad. The ideal for identifying a body would be to have the blood samples of direct ascendants or descendants —parents or children—but it is often the case that no children exist, or no parents any longer, only aunts, uncles and distant cousins.

"I had a case like this, two brothers of sixteen and seventeen, missing in Korazac. In the database, we only had one sample from an aunt, and that was it. It was not enough for identification. Today, with evolving techniques, it can be done with aunts and uncles, but you need several of them. I tried to get in touch with the aunt to know more, but she had changed her number. Impossible to locate her. And so, I left for Korazac, I talked with people, and I eventually found a man who knew her. He informed me that the mother of the two boys was still alive, that there was also a surviving brother and sister, and that they lived somewhere in the United States and had never returned to Bosnia. The guy told me that they all had serious psychological problems. According to him, the mother was in hospital, the brother was an alcoholic and the sister could not be found. He did not know if she had married, or if she had changed her name. In these circumstances, I cannot do anything. My research ends there. But what is sad, is that these two young boys' bodies are maybe somewhere in a morgue, lying there, still waiting after all these years."

With Senem, I had grasped the complexity of her work with bones, the issue of secondary mass graves, of bodies mixed up with each other, all the constraints to be taken into account before getting to the stage of an analyzable DNA sample in a laboratory. Listening to Darija, it was the complexity of the living that seemed to come to the fore, the living who move around, who remain silent, who burn their bridges, who want to forget or who die. Of course, DNA reveals blood ties, but it could not say anything about the quarrels or the bitterness, nothing about the wounds or reproaches, the love exchanged or where opportunities for it have been missed. Darija does not untangle bones; she excavates family stories and the memories of the living.

"Sometimes, Serb families do not want to give their blood in case Muslims handle it. Now that, that makes me angry. I explain to them that no one can know their identity, that all the samples are anonymous, with bar codes. I say: 'Do you not want your son to rest in peace, do you not want a grave to gather around? Do you not think your son deserves this? Rather than lying in the morgue, without an identity?' Sometimes, it makes them change their mind but there are occasions when you can do nothing. They answer me: 'All the earth is hallowed ground, it is not important where he is buried.' I remember a few times, they ended up hanging up the phone on me. The worst is when I am pretty certain we have had the body in the morgue for the last ten or fifteen years, and we just need to identify it."

We head back to the center of town. I have to see Zoran who has promised to bring me a bottle of Rakija before I return back to Emira and Mehmed's house. En route, I share my thoughts with Darija.

"Lots of Serbs think that people only want to talk about what happened to Bosniaks, because of the ethnic cleansing. That there is no place for their suffering. As if there was a hierarchy in the suffering.

"Personally, I have found in all these massacres committed in the name of ethnic cleansing, a hierarchy does already exist. Srebrenica is always talked about, but rarely what happened here, in this region's camps. And that," she pauses, "is really not normal." We walk in silence, then Darija adds:

"It is complicated to talk about it this way, in this general way. You should come and follow me in my work, it would be more simple. You would see for yourself."

2015

8

REPAIRING HUMANS

The bag and the camera tripod weigh heavily on my shoulders as I walk to Šejkovaća morgue. I have left early to be there by 9AM, the time when Senem arrives, and it is already hot, the heat of August that easily hits 100 degrees. I am not used to all this unwieldy equipment and it makes me sweat. The camera bag bumps against my thigh with each step, while the tripod one twists against my back.

For the last six months, I have been learning to make films. I have decided to make one, about Senem and Darija. I found a reason to come back. But right now, here, in the morning sun, I am regretting not having my far lighter pen and notebook.

Yesterday, as I arrived at Sanski Most, it was so hot that I went in search of a place to swim in the surrounding area, by the Sana River which runs the length of the road from Prijedor, then crosses the town. Through the bus window, I had looked longingly at the families sitting with their picnics by the river's edge, the children splashing around in the current, near Čarakovo village, where the river flowed closer to the road. It was a Sunday in August, the air smelt of holidays and lazing around, barbecues on the campfires and chilled beers. I saw Sudbin's house through the apple trees in his garden. I wondered how he was doing.

Arriving in Sanski Most, a taxi driver had dropped me off at the Oaza Motel, an oasis according to its Serbo-Croatian name and, according to Google maps, the closest hotel to the morgue, right on the border of the industrial zone and a suburban neighborhood. As I looked for a way that led to the Sana River, I noticed that there was a public water park nearby, just behind the morgue. The ticket seller at the entrance let me in free because it was due to close in an hour, and I melted into the holiday crowd lounging by the side of the pools, on their deckchairs on the lawn, or under beach huts, the children launching themselves down the slides and the teens pushing each other into the swimming pool, their loud shouts and big splashes piercing the air.

Once my head was under the water, the heat and the fatigue of the journey dissipated, and the late afternoon sun seemed less harsh. I realized that I had never explored this town other than through the morgue, deep in the industrial zone, a stone's throw away from this place of summer sun and fun, children squawking and laughing. Heading back, I passed in front of the morgue's building, the doors shut, and higher up, a few windows were left open.

As I walked towards Šejkovaća in the morning, a thought suddenly became clear to me as I recalled all this summer living right next to the big hangar filled with bones: the dead and the living are not two separate worlds, they belong to the same circle, the human circle. By arranging bones and collecting little drops of blood, Senem and Darija were patiently reweaving this circle, broken when the dead were divested of their dignity, when the living were denied the chance to say a proper goodbye, allowing them to continue to live. For as long as there are people who do this work, who repair that which has been destroyed and trampled upon, something of our humanity is preserved for us all.

When I arrive at the morgue, Senem is already there, seated at her laptop in the trailer, in the middle of a discussion with Ajša. Three white puppies play in front of the entrance, rolling in the grass. They look like cuddly toys. A stray mother dog has selected the kennel as her home and has given birth to a litter.

I set up my camera in the office and I too get to work. Framing the shot requires me to look differently at things and keeps me at a remove, a position that reminds me of my last day here, a year before, when I watched as the placing in the coffins progressed, in a corner of the hangar, for hours, occasionally talking, but more often than not, remaining silent, and observing—as I had at the mass grave, two years previously, taking the time to look, trying to understand, to let the story emerge through the slow elapse of time and repetition.

Senem seems preoccupied, she is going through documents on her computer attached to several hard discs. These contain databases, information on the identifications in progress and those already completed, along with exhumations and autopsy reports. She lights a cigarette, continues to scroll through files on her computer, her smoke in one hand, the computer mouse in the other, ashtray perched on a corner of the desk, next to her sunglasses and her phone, which, because of an updating issue, can't take phone calls today. It irritates her. "Ajša, can you get me the Jakarina Kosa file, please? I cannot find what I'm looking for here... "

Behind Senem is a metallic shelving unit stacked with green and blue files, each indicating a place and time. They are the archives of the different exhumations: Stara Rijeka 1996, Lanište 1996, Hrastova Glavica 1998, Jama Lisac 2000, Jakarina Kosa 2003, Stari Kevljani 2004.... This last one occupies a whole row, given the number of victims that were found in its pit.

For several days, new excavations are being prepared at Jakarina Kosa. The prosecutor's office thinks that there could be more human remains in this secondary grave which served to conceal the Tomašića bodies. The site is in a difficult place to access, on a slope. Senem wants to send an archaeologist to mark the ground, but for this the prosecutor's authorization is required and, as we are deep into the month of August, the prosecutor is on holiday. I get the impression that this too, is an irritation for her.

Ajša puts down the large blue folder on the desk, leans over Senem as she flicks through it, takes out handwritten pages. It is the exhumation report written up in English by the forensic pathologist in charge of the excavations. In the middle of the bundle, a drawing scribbled by hand, a cliff, pine trees, stick figures lying down and a diagram showing where the bodies were discovered.

"Do you understand any of this, Ajša? I can't manage to read this..."

"First bodies... in the... middle of slope—I think that's it, right?"

"And here, five heads, do you see that also?"

"Yes, that's it."

"It is questionable whether these bodies... but is it bodies or bones there?"

Together, they try to decipher the pathologist's crazy writing, it is difficult, Senem sighs. Each detail can be useful for preparing an excavation, but for the moment she does not know what she is looking for. She lights another cigarette.

"Don't make a mess in there!" she blurts out, with a lop-sided grin, when I head towards the hangar, awkwardly dragging my equipment.

"I'll try not to," I answer, barely avoiding jamming myself in the door with my unfolded tripod.

Upon entering the building, I am overwhlemed with emotion. I stand frozen for a moment, the camera in one hand, the tripod in another, waiting to calm down. I allow my eyes to take in the length of walls, the rows of trolleys, the photos of the missing, and I say to myself that this is what I came to film: the beauty of what happens here, what is repaired here. I film the graphic lines of the hangar, all that height up to the ceiling, the light that enters through the windows, the salt and rust marks on the empty trays in the corner, piled against a wall. I zoom in on these traces, they look like maps, seen from above, the salt like sea ice, the grey sea of the tray all around. I remember the summer before, this first room cluttered with green coffins, stacked on top of each other. Today, it is practically empty, as are the majority of the trolleys, stored against the walls. The door that leads to the front awning where Zlatan works is closed, the Kärcher is tidied away next to a pallet in which a dozen bags of salt remain piled up. There is a silence that I have never heard here before. Even the birds have gone silent, it must be too hot for them.

In the evening, I meet Senem in a restaurant on the banks of the Sana. We sit on the terrace overlooking the river. Children play in the water, Senem looks exhausted, tells me she feels heavy, that she has put on weight in the last year. She sighs, "I get tired more quickly. I am trying to diet, but when I feel empty, I fill myself up with food."

Since last summer, she has moved to Sarajevo where she bought an apartment. She is happy with her new home, even if she says she still spends the same amount of time on the road, between Šejkovaća and the morgues that she visits for the N.N. project.

This past winter her mother had some health problems, and now only works part-time. Her father is retired, Senem has worries. "I am fully realizing that I am becoming the parent of my parents. My father has a very small pension and my mother's salary has been reduced by half. I have to make sure they have something to fall back on."

She no longer talks about her wish to grow medicinal plants, and when I ask her the question, she frowns. "This is not the time," she says. I can understand this. It would require money, investment, no, it is really not the time, what with her parents getting old and needing her.

"Instead, I'm thinking of finding a job abroad for a few years, a better paid job than here, to put some money aside. I want to see other things, and what's more I think, for my career, it will be good. Anyway, in Bosnia, nothing will happen in the next two or three years. Since I started running this morgue in 2009, I have the impression that the situation for the missing has got worse, not gotten better. And I would still find work if I came back in a few years."

I sense that she is worn out, I see a lassitude that I have not observed in her before. She had always given me the impression of a person who transforms anger into a kind of fuel to get things done, to tackle obstacles. But now, it is as if she has had enough and no longer wants to battle. She talks at length about the absurdities that she must untangle in the N.N. Project, which was meant to last eighteen months and two years later, is no closer to ending.

"Sometimes I find torn body-bags, bones that have got mixed up, DNA results which are useless because we do not know which body they go with. There is no real will to create a system that works properly, with the required funds to cover it."

She lights a cigarette. I understand her fatigue. It is in the interest of a lot of people for the missing not to be found, that it all continues for ten, fifteen, thirty more years. It is about funds, careers, salaries, even glory when a new mass grave attracts the media, as well as furnishing a weighty political argument. Senem, furious, talks to me again about Tomašića, how some came to swagger in the press spotlight, prompting the contempt of the families who must wait not just to grieve but also to sort out all the administrative formalities. A death certificate issued after identification brings formal status as a widow or an orphan, and various accompanying social benefits.

"You too, you earn your living because of the missing," I point out to her.

"Yes, it's a salary, my career. But that does not give me the right to do whatever I like and to not show respect to the families or the dead. All that interests me, is to successfully identify these anonymous bodies that we are reviewing. In Mostar, of a hundred cases, we have identified thirty. That is huge."

"But if I understand you correctly, that means the number of missing given to us is probably not the whole truth."

"The number of missing declarations made by the relatives are closer to the truth. For the rest... it's a lot more complicated. And this is where we need to put the money at this point, so that we can clarify the maximum number of these cases hanging around for years. Today, it is not that useful anymore to go looking for mass graves. We will certainly find a few more. But that is not where you will find all the bodies. Others are in graves, under false identities, because of mistakes committed during the first few years after the war.

"And for the remainder who lie waiting in morgues, we cannot hang about. People die and those who are still here are distant family members, they are not necessarily concerned in the same way. For a young Swedish boy, it might not interest him to find his great uncle's bones, he knows he disappeared during the war and that is enough for him—what interests him is not burying his great uncle, but where he's going for his holidays! So, either we spare no expense on blood samples while there is still time, or we invest in the analysis of remains in the morgues. But it's crucial that we do something so that this whole issue can come to an end!"

I am reminded of when she was wondering what to do with the bodies, then telling me about her coup with the salt, her sheer determination could only impress me. She was over-whelmed, but she was proud to have pulled it off. Today, I get the sense her work is pushing her to her limit.

"You never told me what it was really like, working on the Tomašića bodies."

"It was really hard for us all. Even if we did not want to ad-mit it. The fact the bodies were in that state, so well preserved... You see, usually we handle bones. Here, we were handling bod-ies, people, human beings, by the hundred. We began at eight AM, we finished at seven or eight PM. We never had lunch, we couldn't manage it, it was too... disgusting."

One night, Senem had a dream. In it, she was at work and she explained to her team: "It's such a shame that we are throw-ing away all this meat!" The next day, she told her colleagues about the dream, they laughed, it became the running joke for several days.

"I do not know how we got through those months. The number of victims was not unlike a plane crash. With a crash you have a team of fifty people, a team for the families, another offering psychological support, one for DNA analysis, a team of pathologists, a press unit... Me, I had a team of eight people to do everything, and the Prosecutor of the Republic of Bosnia-Herzegovina, at the other end of the phone from the Mladić trial at the ICTY[4]."

The Tomašića victims added yet another chapter to this prosecution which has continued for years. Each body was a piece of evidence.

"One morning, like every other morning, I arrived at work before the others to prepare for the day, I went to open the morgue to air it, I had my cup of coffee in my hand, and

---

4. The International Criminal Tribunal for the former Yugoslavia

there, just as I was about to open the doors, I stopped in front of them and thought, 'My god, I am running a factory for the dead.' Because that is what it was really like: a factory. You had to do things like on a production line, and not get it wrong."

For the two months after the last identifications, Senem had nightmares: that people would realize that there were mistakes and all her work would come into question.

There have been none to date.

"I am proud of myself and my team, of all we succeeded in doing together. Before Tomašića, I didn't always feel very sure of myself. Sometimes, I doubted my abilities. But ever since, no longer.

"Yes, I'd say you can be proud of yourself," I say smiling at her.

Around us, night has fallen, the river is lost in the darkness, the children have long gone home. Only the sound of the river can be heard. It is late.

"You know, for me," Senem continues, "the war started on April 9th. I remember it well because it was the day before my birthday. My parents had met up with the neighbors in our living-room to discuss events. Us children, we were sent to the kitchen while the adults talked about what should be done. Together, they decided to protect the women and children. That is how we came to leave for Croatia, on the bus, and when we arrived, we slept in a dormitory. It was my birthday, and all my friends from my neighborhood were there. I had no idea who was what, in terms of religion. I would have been incapable of telling you. It was only afterwards that I understood there were the Croats, the Serbs, the Muslims, the Romanians, the Jews.... Do you see?"

I recognize in Senem's voice that astonishment that I often hear in the accounts about the start of the war, the incomprehension when confronted with a world suddenly tipped into a new order.

The next day, I arrive at the morgue at the same time as Samir, the policeman who guards the site. He opens the doors of the trailer and the morgue, prepares a coffee for himself and me in the little kitchen, turns on the radio and rolls a cigarette, perching on one of the office chairs. We smile at each other for lack of a shared language, after I have exhausted the few words that I know in Serbo-Croatian: Thank you, goodbye, cow, taught to me by Mehmed but not really useful here. I listen to the news with Samir, I grasp a few words, the refugee crisis in the Greek islands, the war in Syria. When I go outside to film, I see one of the puppies, dead, its mother lying by the little thing's side, licking its head. A car must have run it over.

A vehicle parks in front of the hangar. It is Senem arriving with Vladimir, a trainee archaeologist from a Serbian university. She is carrying an enormous bag of dog biscuits for the dogs. Her face looks tired: "I didn't sleep well last night, I think I went to bed too late." Coffee, cigarette, "any milk, Samir?"

"No, no more milk, we finished the carton yesterday," he replies.

"Oh no, she says with a sigh, I hope Ajša brings some when she comes." She opens her laptop, plugs in her hard discs, the steaming cup of instant coffee without milk by the ashtray, in which a slender cigarette burns, as she types her passwords, rubs her eyes.

"Samir, please, can you deal with the dead puppy?"

Then she turns to me: "I cannot handle seeing it like that, with its mother next to it.... " Her expression is somewhere between exhaustion and amusement at what is clearly the absurdity of the situation. "Do you realize Taina, I spend my time with corpses but I am not up to dealing with a dead puppy!" She shakes her head. Samir goes out with a garbage bag to wrap around the animal's body, Ajša arrives with milk, the day is saved.

At lunch, we go and eat together in a simple local eatery, Senem starts her meal with a coffee, everyone laughs at her strange habit. She talks about the diet that she is on, the Dukan diet, which only allows meat protein at the beginning, and I laugh, because that really is the perfect diet for the Balkans!

"By the way, Vlad, did you find the skull?" Senem suddenly blurts out, remembering his task for the morning.

"Yes, but I had to look for it for a long time, opening up the bags. It didn't smell too good."

"Not too good?" Senem bursts out laughing. "Vlad, you've seen nothing yet, you. Compared to the Tomašića bodies, what you smelt there was practically perfume!"

Later, in the morgue, I film her examining a body. With Vladimir, they carry it from the main room towards the examination room and place it on a table. Senem sets up her equipment, a red pen, a yellow highlighter, the osteometry ruler, the form with a skeleton drawn in it, where she will color in each missing bone in red, will note each fracture or crack, the measurement of the femur. I watch her movements through the camera viewfinder, those hands that rummage through a pile of bone debris to find the missing piece of a shattered skull, stick it back in place, then arrange the phalanges of a hand.

"Would it bother you if I put on some music? I like working to music."

No, it does not bother me. She turns on the radio, it is a hit of the moment, "love me like you do, lo-lo-love me like you, touch me like you, tou-tou-touch me like you do…" I watch her take the vertebrae one by one in her hands, arrange them in the right order on the table, and I recognize the hand movements that she showed me when I came into the hangar for the first time. And I remember her phrase also: "Look. The bones tell us about themselves. "

9

FADILA'S GRANDDAUGHTERS

adila welcomes us on the doorstep, her wrinkled face lit up by a big smile, her hand on the doorframe to support herself. "Come in, come in! We shall sit in the living-room." She keeps in front of us, limping as she walks, hand on a painful hip. "Come, come!"

Darija gives me a quick wink. Earlier, in the car, she had warned me. "You'll see, I think she very much wants to talk. It is often like that. People have waited for so long to have somebody listen to them."

"You were the one who called me?" Fadila asks to reassure herself.

"Yes, it was me."

"I thought to myself, 'My goodness, this woman talks so easily!'"

"You know, I meet a lot of people in my work, so I must know how to talk easily with people," Darija says smiling. She walks towards the sofa, puts down her red plastic file on the low table by the tray that Fadila has prepared, with biscuits and two glasses of juice for us. A small fan placed on a chest of drawers in the corner keeps the air circulating.

"Sit down, sit down!"

Two slender adolescent girls suddenly appear from a bedroom to greet us, blond hair in ponytails, shy smiles.

"Are these your granddaughters?" Darija asks.

"Yes, they are thirteen and fourteen years old, only seventeen months between them.

"They look a lot like you!"

"Yes, that is what they say: 'they are their grandmother's granddaughters!' Medina, will you prepare some coffee for us? We cannot have these ladies without coffee."

The young girl disappears into the kitchen, her sister remains with us, looking a bit awkward, in that typical adolescent posture, with a body that has grown so quickly that they don't know what to do with it. Darija smiles at her, perhaps it reminds her of something, as it has me. I unpack the camera, the tripod, the mic, while the teen, who has positioned herself by the fan, observes me out of the corner of her eye. A mixture of curiosity and reserve.

Yesterday morning, I had left Senem to come film with Darija. It was the first time I had followed her in her work. "I'm a bit stressed," she had said to me." I'm worried my hands will shake."

I had tried to reassure her: 'Just do what you usually do,

that will work fine.' But the truth was my own hands were also shaking. I had no idea what to expect, and the camera was challenging me. Some of the images filmed the day before were overexposed and blurred. We had driven to a small hamlet not far from Sanski Most to visit an old woman whose father had disappeared during the war; he had lived in the house where his now-retired daughter was receiving us.

She had very little to tell us: "You understand, I was in Germany when it happened." We had sat down outside, under the green arch of a pergola covered in vine, and Darija had begun her questionnaire. ("Your father's name"; "your mother's name") and I thought about the memories that each of these utterly simple questions could trigger in this seventy-year-old woman: memories of her as a little girl with her parents whom she still called mummy and daddy; her as a newlywed, the happiness shared with her family; then her and her children with their grandfather, the summer holidays spent in this house, the bond between the little ones born in Germany and their grandpa in Bosnia; and then nothing at all, just a terse account of the disappearance: "He was last seen on that little path leading to the forest, that is all we know."

Towards the end of our visit, a neighbor showed up, a plate of steaming bureks in her hands. Darija had politely declined ("otherwise I would put on two kilos a week," she said to me later in the car), but the woman had insisted so much that I had accepted one in her place. I munched on the flaky pastry filled with spiced meat, smiled at the neighbor to let her know how good it was, the two women watching me eat, looking pleased, while Darija rolled a cigarette. As we left, they slipped us two chocolate bars, "for the road."

"It's often like this," Darija had said to me in the car after the visit. "The people know very little. Sometimes, they can tell you where the person was last seen, but that's it."

"As if they had evaporated into thin air," I said.

"Yes, that's it exactly."

"Right Fadila, you know why I have come, don't you?"

Darija's voice is suddenly less breezy, gone are her phrases about the rain and the nice weather which put everyone at ease, it is time to get down to the work. She leans forward on the sofa, to try and catch the gaze of Fadila, who has sat down on the chair opposite.

"Your father disappeared during the war, as well as your two brothers. We found your father, who could be buried, but your two brothers Hazim and Sadik are still reported as missing. Every year, mass graves are found and opened. When this happens, it's important that we have as many blood samples as possible in our database, to identify the people who have been found.

"Thank you for doing this work, for dealing with all this."

"Someone must do it. We started fifteen years ago and we will not stop halfway through. It would not be right unless we have found everyone. Therefore, Fadila, what I am going to do now, is fill in this antemortem questionnaire for your two brothers with you. I will ask you a certain number of questions, about their physical characteristics and the circumstances of their disappearance, and you will answer me if you can..."

From here on in, Darija's tone remains grave, her sentences are extremely clear. She communicates information, instructions. They need to make headway.

"I left them so long ago," Fadila whispers, and her eyes glaze over, the smile has disappeared. I got married in Sanski Most, then I came here, to Gradiška."

"When did you come to Gradiška?"

"When was it now..."

"Was it before the war?"

"Yes, it was before the war. I had two children at the time, and I had two more here. Two boys and two girls."

"Four children in total?"

"That's right. One of my daughters got married, but she died age twenty-five. What to say… it was her fate. I have a son who lives not far from here, and another in Austria. And one daughter in Australia. She and her husband own the house at the end of the road."

"They come in the summer?"

"From time to time, yes. They came for July then left. It's very expensive for them to come, the plane tickets… "

"Fadila, I am going to first fill in the form for Hazim, then for Sadik. Hazim was born in 1961, is that right?"

"Yes, that's right. I remember it because Hazim was born, and then right after, I gave birth to my eldest child."

"How old are you, Fadila?"

"Me? I am seventy now."

"Was Hazim married?"

"Yes, he had two sons, who are grownups now. He lived in Čarakovo, and worked as a security guard in Prijedor. My God, what a hard worker he was, Hazim."

"It was Hazim who disappeared the same day as your father, or was it your other brother, Sadik?"

"That was Sadik. With Hazim, it was his former schoolmates who took him away, and he never came back. He had just enough time to say to his wife, 'Take care of the children.'"

"Did you hear about where they might have taken him? What happened to him? Any sort of story?"

"People say they got to Prijedor Bridge, there were a lot of people from Čarakovo with him, and that was there they…"

Fadila breaks off, her trembling voice fails her, but Darija does not allow the silence to take over, she pursues it, they must keep going, overcome the pain brought up by the questions.

"Near the bridge?"

"Yes."

"Are you thinking of the bridge by the Prijedor Hotel?"

"No, the one further on, on the road to Sanski Most. That is where they supposedly forced them to jump off the bridge. At least, that is what I have heard said. I don't know any more than this, my child, I was here."

"Yes, I know you were here, Fadila."

Darija's voice is controlled, reassuring, she will not allow emotions to take over. "I just want to know if there was a story around Hazim's disappearance," she adds.

"I do not know, my child. Where they took them afterwards, or where their bodies are. Only God knows.... I hope that one day, we will know."

"That is our goal. To find people, to restore their name to them, so that they can be buried and rest in peace."

"Yes... That's how my father was found. He had gone to the shop, the shop just on the right, when you come into Čarakovo. Someone shot him in the back. He fell into the Sana River, they only found a part of his head and his hand... it's... what can one say about all this? We buried what was found of him in Čarakovo cemetery. My nephew is buried in there as well, they are side by side."

Fadila's granddaughter has quietly seated herself at the end of the sofa, in the line of the camera, at which she is taking a sidelong glance. I catch her eye in the lens for a brief instant, then her gaze is drawn by the story that her grandmother is telling Darija. She listens in silence, her eyes flit from one to the other, utterly absorbed, eagerly awaiting bits of information or anecdotes that have not been revealed to her about this war that she never knew. This is all to do with her great-grandfather, and her two great uncles, basically prehistory when you are thirteen years old, and yet, all of a sudden, these events seem to come alive again on her grandmother's face.

"God willing, we will find your two brothers, so that they too, can rest in peace," Darija says, keeping the conversation going. "Tell me, Fadila, your brother Hazim, how tall was he?"

"He was tall, yes..."

"Six foot? Or more?"

"Yes, that sounds right..."

"And his hair, what color was it?"

"It was brown, curly hair. He was so handsome, and such a hard worker, my goodness! He was very good with his hands, an intelligent man."

"So, brown, curly hair. Was it short hair?"

"Yes, short hair. He would come and see me sometimes, but not very often, he had his work."

"Yes, he had work commitments. Tell me, can you remember if he was right or left-handed?"

"Right-handed, I seem to remember."

"Did he wear glasses?"

"No, no."

"A smoker?"

"Hazim, no, but Sadik, yes."

"Do you know how he was dressed when they took him away?"

"How could I know, my child, I was not there! His wife might know that but she lives in Germany, she remarried."

"Would you have a photo of either of your brothers?"

"No, I have nothing left. I had some before."

"Was it during the war that you lost them... the photos?"

"Yes, I was a refugee."

Fadila's sentence sums up all that she will not be able to tell us, all those things that get left behind, that will never again be found, when people say it is 'lost forever' or 'we took nothing', because it is a matter of saving yourself and your loved ones first. After having spent several months accompanying Darija with the families, I have come to understand the treasure that a photo represents, when held out to her, it is like a vestige of life from before. Often, when filming these interviews that seem like excavations of memory, as precise and clinical as the excavation of a mass grave, I would think about all that has disappeared along with the destroyed or stolen objects from houses that were ransacked or pillaged: the tales, the anecdotes, the little stories that people tell when taking hold of such objects ("those were your grandmother's cups"; "that was your great-grandfather's watch.") and the words that inevitably follow ("Your grandmother, she loved beautiful things"; "He bought that watch with his first salary.").

But for the time being, in Fadila's sitting room, I understand just a few words, slika, rat, ništa. The dialogue unfolds in front of my camera without any translation, and it is only that, once alone with Darija in the car, I can get a more precise idea through the summaries that she gives me. The true tenor of the exchanges will only be picked up quite a bit later, once Zoran will get hold of the hours of rushes and, minute after minute, will restore the meaning in French to me, of words spoken, the hesitations. For the moment, behind the camera, I can only rely on my eyes to read the gestures, the postures, the sighs, and when that invisible forcefield comes around us, like a mist that becomes ever more dense with each new question from Darija, a language not communicable by words but by how a gaze lights up or becomes more somber.

"Hello, is anyone there?"

A man of about fifty comes in, Fadila addresses him with a smile: "Ah, Fadil, come in!" Then turning towards Darija: "This is my oldest son, the one born just two months after his uncle. The girls' father." After the usual greetings and introductions, Fadil takes a seat, and Darija gets back to her questionnaire: "Did Hazim have any fractures or amputated limbs, and his teeth, how were they, did he have any false teeth?"

"No, he was in good health, Hazim, and so skilled with his hands, he repaired motorbikes, cars, he could turn his hand to so many things."

"And Sadik, what was he like?"

"He was thinner than Hazim," Fadila's son explains. "He was not married."

"Your aunt whom I met explained to me that he was a little... he could work and everything, but..."

"He understood everything," Fadila says, cutting Darija off.

"Yes, but he was a bit, how does one say..." Darija repeats, searching for the words that would be the most appropriate, giving Fadila an opportunity to complete the sentence.

"He hid in the cellar with the women and children," Fadila says, changing the subject. "They came to get him there. It was my brother Hazim's wife who told me, she was there with him. She told me he was crying. 'Don't let them take me away!', he was shouting. But they took him and no one ever saw him again."

"It was the 23rd of July 1992, that is correct?" asks Darija.

"Yes, that's right."

"Could you describe Sadik to me? His hair color, his height..."

"He was brown-haired. He was.... maybe 180 lbs."

"Did he wear glasses?"

"No, no glasses."

"Did he smoke?"

"Yes, how he liked to smoke! It ruined his teeth. He liked cigarettes more than food!"

"Did he have dentures?"

"No, just blackened, bad teeth."

"Did he have any health problems?"

"He had problems with his nerves, he was seeing the doctor for that."

"Any amputations, fractures?"

"No, nothing."

Darija's hand writes down every reply, ticks the boxes, turns over the page, to the next question, "beard or moustache," "left or right-handed," a relentless litany that summarizes an individual into a list of physical details. No one cares about a talent for mechanics or nervous problems, bones tell us nothing about these kinds of things. Yet these are the recollections that flash up in people's memories, "take care of the children," "don't let them take me away." Later on, when I reread Zoran's translation, I will think of Hazim's young wife, who saw the two brothers go, one after the other, a woman who found herself a widow with two children, her sole legacy the missing brothers' final words.

"Hazim's eldest son, Elvis, he was always with his dad," remembers Fadila. "Ever since his father's disappearance, he has been sick, the poor boy. He chain-smokes, forgets to eat. The younger one, he was only a year old. He has no memory of it. It is my sister Ajša who helps them. Each time she comes from Germany, she brings a car full of provisions for them. Their mother has remarried, she doesn't care one bit about her sons."

"She became a widow very young," Darija says, trying to soothe things. "She sought refuge elsewhere, that is all. Let us not criticize her."

"Yes, it's true," Fadila admits.

"And you, you live around here, right?" Darija asks, addressing the son.

"Yes, the house just behind, with my four children. Their mother abandoned us."

"Are you serious?"

"Yes, I am serious. She left, with our fifth child, the youngest. Anyway, what can we do, with everything we have lived through here, how could a marriage work?"

His voice is bitter. The two teens say nothing. Medina comes out of the kitchen with the coffee, her sister, sitting on the edge of the sofa, stares into space. They were born well after the war, but their father's words bring them irrevocably back to it, their mother's absence is the war's fault, their father's bitterness as well. It is too much trauma, too much pain for the next generation to be spared from it.

"A final thing, Fadila," Darija asks, picking up the thread, wanting to bring back the discussion onto more neutral territory "I need your signature in these documents, to say that you consent to the blood sample I am going to take."

"My child, I never went to school, I cannot read or write."

"It is not a problem, you can leave a fingerprint."

"At the time, it was always the boys who were sent to school, my sister went as well, but for me, as the oldest, I was needed at home, to look after the cows. We were told: 'One of you can go,' so I said to my sister, 'you go, I will stay.' That is how it was, my dear, but well, all things pass...."

"You did not miss anything by not going to school. You have lived a long time, you had your children... Look, you are going to put your print here, there you are. And now, I shall take the blood sample. Could you hold out your hand."

"Just my hand? I thought you would take blood from a vein."

"No, no, an index finger will do. It is just four drops of blood, it will be quick."

Fadila's hand is pale and wrinkled, a hand that has carried, cooked, wiped, comforted, a hand that has looked after cows instead of writing out school lessons. "I don't have very good circulation," she apologizes when Daria sticks a needle into her index finger.

"Don't worry, it will be fine. There you are, turn your palm downwards, this way so I can press on your finger and take four drops."

Silence descends, the moment has something solemn about it, it is the one tangible action that Fadila can undertake to help find her two brothers. The teenagers watch, the four drops of blood bring into a focus a wait that has lasted more than twenty years, these four drops of hope, the color of dark red, which dry on the card that Darija will put away in a sealed envelope. A few months later, I will go to the laboratory where the cards will be punched, the drops of blood analyzed to extract a DNA profile, represented on a computer screen by a row of vertical bars in several colors, this the sum of an identity. These sequences in turn will be compared to the profiles of bone samples analyzed in another laboratory, the one that adjoins Darija's office in Banja Luka which reduced the bone to white powder, before they too were transformed into vertical bars on a computer screen. The final phase, that of comparison, seems incredibly simple, results are run through a computer program in the database and the answer appears on the screen in a matter of seconds when there is a match: a 99.95% probability or more of a blood tie between one profile and another. Below this percentage, a family's uncertainty must continue.

"A little juice? Help yourself to a glass of juice."

Darija has taken off her blue gloves, refused the biscuits,

has asked permission to light a cigarette, has accepted a coffee, just a half cup, served by Medina. I have left the camera to sit down next to Darija on the sofa, and my perspective and position have changed in the cramped space of the living-room, I notice the little placemats in white lace under the television and on the shelves, it makes me think of Emira and Mehmed's house.

Fadila's face has regained its smile, the silence is broken, the conversation begins again, about more trivial things—the weather, the water cut-offs—then turns towards politics: how the young generation born after the war are fed on a diet of nationalism cultivated by the political parties, "whereas before, it was different." Darija rolls a cigarette and nods in agreement, tells how she herself is the product of a mixed marriage, a Serb father, and a Croat mother, that it was not a problem for anyone before the war, that they are still together. Fadila approves, her Ismet has also married a girl whose father is Serb, and it is fine, they get on so well, have had two children. It does not matter to which God you pray, all this drama about nationalism comes from crazy minds.

"And you, do you have children?" Fadila suddenly asks Darija.

"No, no, I am not married. I will leave it up to fate!"

"I hope you find happiness, my child. You are young and beautiful, you will find it. You are someone who is good. When you called me, that is what I thought: this is a good person."

Then she sighs, a long sigh heavy from the weight of the years: "All this, makes me remember so many things, my child… After your phone call, I cried so much."

10
IT GETS UNDER YOUR SKIN, THE JOB

"I was more relaxed this time" Darija tells me in the car after we leave Fadila's house, who stands at her door, waving us off. Darija beeps back and calls out goodbye to her from the car window.

"I tried to do it as if you weren't there," she continues, looking relieved, her hands on the steering wheel. The houses in Gradiška file past us on both sides, we have about an hour's drive before we get to Banja Luka. She lights the cigarette rolled earlier for the trip.

"I am often asked the question about kids," she says taking a drag of her cigarette. "People are surprised: 'how can such a young and beautiful woman like you have no children or husband?' And they suggest suitors!" She laughs with her husky voice. Then she summarizes everything that I have not understood earlier, the story about Hazim's wife who got married in Germany, the girls' mother who left them.

"In fact, you're always caught up in people's family stories."

"It is a bit like that, yes," Darija replies. "Sometimes, DNA testing reveals that the declared father is not the biological father. These are delicate situations. The team, we know, but we cannot talk about it. We just have to find new donors in the family."

I think about the extent to which she must delve into families' intimate details with her questions which, that said, are very simple. I reflect on the words unsaid, the secrets, the resentments, the tightrope walker's skill she must use, between listening and detachment, between empathy and reserve, because she is not there to play at being a psychologist but to fill in a questionnaire.

"Did you receive any training when you started, or advice, about how to deal with all this?"

My question unleashes a huge burst of laughter from her.

"Not a thing! I do what I can, that is all."

The road unfolds, leading us past fields, a village, always the same houses with the sloping roofs, a corner shop, a bakery whose name I can now recognize: Pekara.

"Some of the stories are unbelievable," Darija says. "There was one that really stayed with me. It was fifteen years ago, right at the beginning of the ICMP's activities in Bosnia. With my colleagues, we had contacted the parents of a young man reported as missing, to take a DNA sample. They refused. We called them back several times to chase them up, to explain it all, to try to understand what was stopping them. The father ended up asking us to leave them alone, and to respect their decision. That is what we did, but we never understood why they refused. Then the father died, maybe five years ago. A few years after that, the mother died in turn. At that moment, the uncles of the young man got in touch with us. They wanted to know if they could give their blood, if it could help to identify their missing nephew. We tell them that it is possible and we meet them. They explain to us that the missing boy was an only child and his mother had sworn to her husband that she would kill herself if she learnt her son was dead. For her, he was still alive, somewhere, perhaps in a prison in Serbia or Croatia.

There were lots of rumors like that after the war. But the most unbelievable part of this story," Darija continues as she adjusts her sunglasses, "was that the father, he actually knew the truth. He had come to the morgue to identify his son amongst several bodies. But he had never filled in the paperwork, and above all, never said anything to his wife. They lived together for the rest of their lives, and the husband died taking his secret to the grave. His wife, she had regularly received anonymous phone calls, people who said: we know where your son is, give us money, and we will give you the information. She died with the hope that her son was still alive. The uncles knew the whole story, but they too, never said anything to the mother, they respected the father's decision. Yet once both of them had died, they wanted certainty about what had happened and they contacted us. That is how the son was finally able to be identified. His body had lain waiting in the morgue at Banja Luka for twenty years."

"That is terrible," I say. "The price this man paid to protect the one he loved… And moreover, is it really love, if you have to leave your child in the morgue, without a grave?"

"I don't know," replies Darija, before going quiet as if silence is the only valid response when faced with this story. Then she adds: "No one can know."

She is certainly right. Like so many of the other stories that one hears here, no one can understand the choices that another makes. One can observe the consequences, guess at the cost, but their meaning, if there is one, stays hidden.

"Have you ever been scared?" I ask, changing the subject.

"Scared, no. But one time, I sensed I was in danger. It was a Serb who lived in Croatia, his brother had disappeared. I had driven to his house to take a blood sample. On the phone, he was normal, but when I arrived, I found him completely drunk, in the middle of an argument with his neighbor, spitting at him. He did not even say hello. He yelled, "Come into the house!" and when I went in, he began to talk about the war, his injuries, he ripped off his clothes to show me, then he started on the guns he owned. He got them out of cupboards, all the while continuing to drink. It lasted for three hours, and I was wondering how I would be able to calm him down and take the blood. When he got out the weapons, I thought to myself this could really turn difficult. His wife was there, but she was not going to be the one to stop him, he was yelling at her as well. I finished up by suddenly blurting out: 'What kind of house is this, it has been three hours that you have been drinking down Rajika in front of me and you haven't even offered me a glass!' It had an immediate calming effect on him. He asked his wife to go and get the best Rajika in the house. I drank two glasses with him and I was able to take the two blood samples. When I left, the guy hugged me, crying and saying he hoped I would find his brother."

"And you really weren't scared?"

"No, I was angry! I had driven more than four hundred kilometers to see this man, I had come all this way for him and I certainly wasn't going to leave empty-handed. Anyway, fear is not a very constructive emotion."

We are nearing Banja Luka, the landscape is becoming more urban: industrial buildings, a shopping mall, apartment blocks. I film the road in front of me, the entrance into town, the streets lined with trees, Darija's face in profile, her hands on the wheel, her determined gaze.

"It gets under your skin, this job," she says. "I cannot imagine doing anything else. I like being on the road. At the beginning there were more of us and then, bit by bit, our numbers were reduced and I became team leader in a team that was just me," she says laughing. "But it does not bother me. I like my independence. Hey, do you remember the case I told you about yesterday, the old lady whose disappearance no one had ever flagged, but whose traces I found in the old Red Cross registers? For several days I have been searching to see if she still has family, I've been calling people left and right. Well, what do you know, this morning, a man from her village called me back to give me the number of this woman's nephew! He lives in Bristol, England. I will open a file now and we can ask the nephew for a sample of blood."

Her voice is triumphant, a big smile lights up her face. It is as if she holds these cases even more dear than the others. She calls them the "invisible missing," not declared anywhere, deprived of any existence, even that of a missing person. It is often those cases involving the elderly people, who are childless, who stayed in their villages when everyone else was fleeing. Once the war was over, no one took any steps to find them. Sometimes their bodies lie waiting in a morgue, amongst the N.N. cases that Senem tries to resolve with her team.

In the evening, I meet Darija for a ćevapi, "the best in town," she says. The little snack bar does not look like much but the ćevapi are delicious. We eat them with our fingers, the little grilled spiced sausages, the round shaped white bread, nicely warm. The heat outside is sweltering, in spite of the late hour, and the cool Nektar beer never tasted so good.

"I love beer when it gets hot like this," Darija says. She talks to me about her little niece whom she looks after a lot, about her hesitancy to have a child as a single person, about the abandoned puppy that she found in the forest during a hike with a friend, "We have shared care of the puppy now," she laughs. In turn, I tell her about my family, and how for the last year, I have been learning to put us all back together, the children, the stepchildren, how we are now six in the house. The waitress, who is also the cook and the owner—she runs the little shack on her own—arrives holding a camera: "Can I? It's for our Facebook page." So we pose, giggling like teenagers, clutching our beers.

"This place here, has always been a ćevabdžinica," Darija explains. "During the war, the owner had to leave Banja Luka with his Muslim family. But his daughter returned and re-opened the place, and as you can see, the diners returned as well."

Around us, all the tables are occupied, families, couples, groups of friends, people who have left work. Each day, the Facebook page is filled with new photos.

As we leave, Darija suggests another beer on the banks of the Vrbas River. We walk in the night towards the river, she shows me the Ferhadija great mosque, destroyed during the war, reopened only two months before, for Eid, after fifteen years of reconstruction.

"The day it was destroyed, it was like a part of me disappeared. It was a five hundred-year-old mosque. They demolished the lot, all the town's mosques, but this one, was the oldest. I was used to hearing the call to prayer in the neighborhood, then there was nothing, just the silence."

I understand what she is saying. I grew up in a Muslim country where, as a child, I measured time not by the hands of a watch but by the muezzin calling prayers. That silence would be as if time had stopped.

"I'm no fool," Darija says, once the bottle of Nektar has been opened on the terrace at the water's edge. "I can't be fooled when it comes to these invisible missing."

"What do you mean?"

"I know very well with each case that I find, another name is added to my list, and in a certain way, that justifies my work. And I know that my boss would prefer that the list get shorter rather than longer!"

At the next table, a group of fifty-something friends drink beers, and like us, are recounting anecdotes that I cannot understand, that make them burst into loud laughter. Darija casts them an amused glance, "Ladies Night," she says and we both smile. She rolls a cigarette, lights it up, looks me straight in the eye: "I'm no fool, I know how things work, but I don't care. I'm a pain in the ass!" and she flashes such a wide smile that it crinkles up her eyes.

2020

11

WATER FLEAS AND BUTTERFLIES

The rain comes down in huge drops against the train windows, tracing oblique rivulets the length of the pane. The sky shows no sign of clearing, the clouds huddle on the sides of the surrounding mountains and seem to have stopped moving. My return journey to Paris will be a rainy one. It is the evening, and at the border, the engine change takes longer than usual, unless it is some sort of customs issue or a passport being checked. It is always at this exact point that I have the impression that my journey is about to begin, or come to an end, depending on which way I am crossing the border. I am going home with hard disks full of images, and a wish to return soon to film some more.

The day before, I had spent a last day with Darija in Kostajnica, near this same border, with a Serb family, for a case that was a little unusual: it concerned the re-opening of a file on fifty-five Serb soldiers executed during the war, whose bodies were returned to their relatives in 1995, six months after their deaths. All but four had been recognized by their families, without DNA analysis, except, twenty years on, when international justice cast a closer eye on this mass execution and ordered DNA tests to confirm one of the victim's identity, the outcome caught everyone by surprise: the results and the declared identity of the victim did not match. During the investigation, it turned out the body that they were looking for was one of the four that had been lying waiting in the morgue for twenty years.

"As a result, we now have to start from scratch, we are doing DNA tests for each case," Darija had explained, as we drove towards the Una River marking the border.

We turned left just before the police station and customs post and arrived at the courtyard of a small apartment block. A little girl of around ten came down first, hurtling down the steps, with the round cheeks of childhood, an impish look and long blond hair down her back. She watched us with curiosity, torn between shyness and an impatience to know why we were there. Then a woman appeared, it is her that we have come to see: Slobodanka, accompanied by her mother and her elder daughter, and with a plastic bag in her hand, out of which she got a carton of fruit juice, two glasses and a packet of biscuits, and set all out on the large table in the courtyard. Always the hospitality. They sat down on either side of Darija on the bench, who explained the situation again to them, already disclosed on the phone: Slobodanka's father was one of the fifty-five, he had been identified by traditional methods, without the DNA analysis now required to confirm that an error had not been committed.

"You are his daughter," Darija says addressing Slobodanka, "Therefore we need a sample of your blood. Your mother to whom I spoke already on the phone has informed me that you live in Serbia but you would be here during the summer holidays. This is why I have come."

Slobodanka's expression is one of incredulity, so much information in such few sentences, an old story from twenty years ago that suddenly needs to be unearthed, while she had been trying to grieve her father all this time. She lit a cigarette and let her mother answer Darija's questionnaire—height, weight, hair, amputations, teeth condition—as she stared into nothingness, the wreaths of her cigarette smoke veiling her eyes. She was nineteen years old when her father died, leaving an empty seat in church at her marriage. He was not there for the birth of her three children, nor for each Christmas Eve or end-of-term school play. So many events, each year, to remind her of her father's disappearance. I observe her face through the lens and for a moment feel awkward to look at her in this way, I am protected by the camera, she is exposed to my gaze. I felt the same violence when I was at the Tomašića mass grave, confronted with the grieving families who'd come to find a relative.

During all this time, during the explanations, the questionnaires, the documents to sign, the taking of the blood sample, the little girl has remained seated immobile opposite her mother, observing the scene in total silence. All around the world, parents' pain transforms children into these invisible statues, who wait obediently for their mothers to put back on their mommy faces, the face that asks the little girl to serve the juice to guests once the blood has been taken, or to open a packet of biscuits, then break into a quick smile for her, prompting the little girl to smile back, relieved.

Darija has put away her papers, the envelope with the four drops of blood and has taken out her brown leather tobacco pouch, her little silver colored metal box for filters, and begins her own ritual for the end of a visit. "A whole procedure," she joked in front of Slobodanka, who lights another cigarette herself.

"I don't smoke, so I'm going to have a biscuit," I said in

English and went to the bench to sit down. I, too, have my ritual: a cup of coffee, a glass of juice, the warm burek, the chocolate-filled biscuit, the glass of Rajika. Accepting the hospitality offered to me, visit after visit, house after house.

The border police open the train compartment, "Your papers, please." I hold out my Finnish passport. Outside, the rain continues, the first real rain since I have arrived. I take a sandwich from my bag prepared by Emira earlier with a pear from her garden. After leaving Darija, I stopped off in Trnopolje. Mirela was also there, on holiday at her parents'. I felt like I was with family. We all sat on the terrace, for coffee, to share news, to reconnect, to be together. In the evening, I suggested that we go to dinner at Stara Bašta, in Kozarac: "I'm inviting you, it has been so long." Everyone agreed. I was happy to be able to give something back, I, who for so long had been coming here, always finding a bed with clean sheets, bread for breakfast left on the table when I was leaving at the crack of dawn, a pita od jabuka (apple pie) baked the day before with the fruit gathered from the garden by Mehmed.

At Stara Bašta, we ate too much grilled meat, as always; we listened to the two singers perform their concert at full volume, as always, so loud that we could not hear each other unless we shouted so much that it made us hoarse the next day. Mehmed was singing, Emira and Mirela too, all the songs that I am beginning to recognize, having heard them in the bars, the buses and the nights at Stara Bašta. Emira's smile was so wide it made her eyes smile too, and I was happy to see her like this, taking her husband's hand to sway to the rhythm of the music, letting life wash away, for a brief instant, all that had been difficult and harsh.

This morning, she had prepared breakfast for Mirela and me, and next to the cup of steaming coffee, she had placed a rose picked from her garden. "This is for you," she said to me. "For your marriage this summer."

Mirela grumbled, joking: "Me too, I want one!."

Emira kept saying in a firm tone: "Only for the bride!"

Two hours later I left for the Tomašića mass grave accompanied by Mirela. We had not planned it. I had lost the desire to film the site, the result of spending time with Senem and Darija, as if the story was with these two women now, and no longer at the mass grave. Then I got frightened that I would regret not going, and Mirela offered to come. "In any case, I was looking for a reason to go," she said to me.

We spent an hour and a half looking for the place. My recollections were too vague. I had not written down any GPS coordinates, and exhumation sites are not listed on Google Maps. The directions given by the few people we came across on the road led us through many a detour to Tomašića village, and the closer we got to the village, the more complicated it became. Where exactly were we going in Tomašića? To the mine? To somebody's house? No, no, we are looking for a mass grave, the one that was found there in 2013. Faces went blank, no one knew about it, had never heard of it, were not from around here. The absurdity of the situation made us both laugh.

Mirela ended up changing our strategy. "Get your camera out," she said to me. "Put it on your knees so it can be seen, it will look serious." Then she stopped people: "Hello, I am accompanying a journalist, we are searching for the Tomašića mass grave, do you know it?" Two young women on bikes gave us clear directions, to the small bumpy track in the mist that I had taken two years previously.

At the end of the trail, there was a pretty little lake. The pit bordered by mounds of earth had filled with water, attracting water fleas and butterflies, dragonflies perched on reeds swaying in the wind. Traces of animal footprints were visible in the clay-like soil, roe deer perhaps, that had come to drink. All was still, tranquil, despite the thunder that rumbled in the distance. There was no horror, no smell, it was just a simple lake with tadpoles, as peaceful as any country landscape. I thought about Senem, about the bodies that I had seen come out and be lined

up on wooden planks right on this muddy soil, the air preg-
nant with that smell, this earth whose entrails we had opened
up to bring forth bodies that it had never managed to digest. It
was now done. Someone had forgotten a faded piece of a police
marker on the orange-hued soil, it was the only vestige of the
months of digging, with the shovels and the digger that had
turned over the earth countless times, and whose marks I knew
were there, hidden by the color of the ground, the morphology
of the landscape, the relief of the now metamorphosed land. I
watched the fleas flit on the water's surface, the trajectory of a
dead leaf propelled by the wind, and I thought to myself that
nature did not need as much time as humans to heal wounds.

Mirela did not approach the water. She kept her distance,
standing on a mound of earth like I had during my week on the
site two years earlier, contemplating the landscape in silence,
hands in her trouser pockets. Her slender silhouette stood out
against an ever more menacing sky, the clouds rolling by on the
wind.

The train starts moving as dusk falls, the rain does not cease.
Suddenly, I very much want to be at home, to have returned
the camera, the tripod and mics, an overwhelming desire to be
in my home with my loved ones. I close my eyes and I see the
story of the film being born, a story about two strong women
who work with their hands, who make the dead and the living
speak, who light cigarettes, lots of cigarettes. I see the reeds, the
water fleas, the animal traces on the muddy earth, a story about
what remains in our hands once war draws away, but without
ever really ending.

Six months later, when I have received a writing grant for
my film, I learn that Senem has just been recruited by the ICRC,
the International Committee of the Red Cross. She writes to me
from Kabul, in Afghanistan, where she has been deployed for
two years. A few days later we talk on Skype.

"You know Taina," she says to me, "I think by coming here

I was able to understand how much my work in Bosnia is linked to who I am, to my own story. When I was there, I could not see it. Here, I have a lot to learn, and in a certain way, it is so much simpler."

2016

12

THE MISSING SOLDIER

The car slams to a standstill in front of the semi which looms from around the bend, suddenly taking up the narrow road between the cliffs that tower to the left and the Una River to the right, below us. My camera narrowly misses smashing against the dashboard, but Darija retains a stoical calm. "The road is a little dangerous, I told you," she explains and reverses a few meters back to allow the trucks to negotiate the bend. "In winter I try to avoid this route. With the black ice and the snow... you see."

I am relieved that it is only November and the snow has only fallen above on the heights.

Since my last journey a year ago, Darija has cut her hair. No longer is there a blond bun atop her head, her hair now falls to her shoulders in a ponytail held by her sunglasses which she pushes up on her forehead. It suits her. I film her in profile while the truck finishes up its maneuver, like a large and cumbersome caterpillar, passing us with a beep of the horn to say thank you. Darija responds with a wave.

Her face shows worry. This morning when I met her at her office, I was surprised by the corridor's silence. "The DNA laboratory has closed, do you remember?" she said. It was true that she had mentioned it in a message, but I had not expected this ghostly atmosphere where, the summer before, the sound of colleagues' footsteps could be heard in the hall, their laughs in the break room, the hum of machines grinding bone samples.

"It's sad, isn't it," she blurted out, preparing coffee in the little kitchen. "Even the heating has been cut. I had to bring in an electric heater to not freeze." She is worried about the future. Her employer has announced that that there will probably be other redundancies. The ICMP budget relies heavily on what each state donates to it. They choose the projects that they want to finance, and in 2016, the Balkans' missing are frankly no longer a priority, as opposed to Iraq or Syria.

"Actually, do you have any news from Senem?" I ask Darija, who has lowered her sunglasses to shield her eyes from the blinding light that awaited us around the bend.

"Yes, we talk on Messenger from time to time, things seem to be working out, she was so sick of this country..."

"And you? Have you had enough as well?"

"At times, but not to the point of leaving," she says with a smile.

"Her team miss her a lot in Visoko. I hope that she will come back for the holidays next summer and we can go to our island in Croatia as usual."

"She told me about that place. She loves it, I think you do as well."

"Yes, it's a hidden spot, in the middle of nature, by the sea, not another soul. I love the calm of nature, even more now with the passing years."

The car speeds along the narrow road which zigzags through the bottom of the canyon. I think back to Senem's face, which I had spotted in the morgue at Visoko. She was smiling from a photo printed on an A4 sheet taped to the pale green tiles of the examination room, next to some post-it notes with some of her colleagues' in-jokes. Senem had been their boss. By her face, someone had stuck a little red-paper heart.

I miss her as well. I have the impression that she has left a void in this story that I am trying to film, and I am not sure if anyone else will fill it. I had to discover the N.N. group which she had spoken to me about so much, without her. I filmed the eight people at work, the bones brought out of a body bag and arranged in order on an examination table, with always the same hand movements, some defter than others depending on experience. Salih's movements are quick and precise, he has been doing it for fifteen years. They call him the bone wizard of the team.

Then there are Amina Victoria's hand movements, still hesitant. She is a young intern of around twenty, from England, where she was born to parents who survived the ethnic cleansing. She chose forensic anthropology, as if to repair this country that is her own but in which she did not grow up. "Can't say I was sure that I was going to work here at the end of my studies," she had admitted to me. But in order to learn the hand movements capable of bringing order to a jumble of bones, this is the area that she chose to work in. I had observed them through my camera lens, able to recognize some of the faces that I had come across at the Tomašića mass grave three years earlier, faces that concentrated on their work, laughed during the lunch break, expressed goodwill to each other. They made me think of a family, each in their place, but in the middle, the empty space left by Senem.

To get to Ostrožac village, you must turn off to the right,

cross the river and go up towards the cliff opposite, on a road of hairpin bends for five kilometers. As we rise away from the canyon below, I catch sight of it through the trees. The landscape is striking. I did not grow up in the mountains, their steep and jagged lines always provoke a feeling of anxiety in me.

Darija stops at a bakery shop to ask for directions: "Yes, it's here, on the other side of the road, just a little further along."

Husnija opens the door to us. He is an old bald man in a checked shirt and a brown sweater, wool socks on his feet. In the dining room, his wife is sitting on one of the sofas, wearing a headscarf, a cane in her hand and a tartan rug over her lap. She apologizes for not getting up to greet us, her joints are painful, and at eighty, she struggles to walk. Her voice has a plaintive tone. She reminds me of my grandmother, a Finnish country-woman, small and round, always in a headscarf as well, her feet in woollen socks that she herself knitted. Here as there, you take off your shoes before entering a house. Here as there, the first thing that you are offered after taking off your shoes and entering, is a coffee and a little something to eat. Today, it is a chocolate sponge cake covered in whipped cream.

"This is my son, he has come to help serve the coffee." A man of about fifty, tall and thin, almost bald like his father, greets us with a smile, then busies himself in the kitchen set in the corner of the living-room: there is water to boil, the coffee to measure into the traditional Turkish enamel cafetiere. It is a red and white polka-dotted one in this house.

"We will have coffee first and then do the work afterwards," Husjina suggests.

"Perfect, and while we wait for the coffee, I will explain the situation to you. I have already spoken to you about it on the phone, but I will explain it in more detail." Darija has no intention of losing grip of the situation. She needs to lead the interview, she knows what she has come to get.

"Did you go and see my little niece in Bihać?" Husnija asks.

"Yes, I have indeed met Semira. I do not know the reason why her brother Samir's disappearance was not recorded in our database. He disappeared when he was a soldier in the Bosnian army, and the information should have automatically been transferred to our records. This was not the case, I do not know why exactly. We realized our mistake when the investigators at the Missing Persons Institute compared our lists with those of the army and we found your nephew's name. We therefore made contact with Semira whom I went to see in Bihać. She gave me information about her brother and I took a blood sample. The problem is that we need several family members in order to identify the DNA.

"She has nobody, the poor kid. Neither a brother nor a sister. She only has me, her uncle."

"That's right. She just has you. That is the reason why I have contacted you: You are her uncle and your blood can identify Samir."

"If it's not too late already…"

"It is never too late. It is possible that Samir's body has already been found and he is in a morgue, but without an identity. This is what we call the N.N. cases. And what's more, we find new mass graves every year. Samir disappeared in the Grabež region, correct?"

"Yes, he was on leave with two soldiers, they fell into an ambush by the Serb army. Ever since, not one bit of news. We have heard a lot of things said, that he might have been hanged, or shot, or thrown into the Una River. If that is the case, we have no chance of finding him one day."

"No, it is possible. It does happen that we find bodies thrown into the rivers. We have had several cases like that."

"That something like this should never happen again…"

"Yes. It is all that we can hope for. And we must do everything possible to find these poor people and bury them with dignity, so they can rest in peace. Tell me, do you know the family on the side of Samir's father, Sulejman? I searched for information, but I couldn't find anything."

"Unlike us, they are from Pećigrad. But they are all deceased."

"Right. Then we shall try with your sample and Semira's."

"And Semira's children?"

"That is another branch of the family again. But as we have his sister's sample, that will be enough for the moment."

Husnija is doubtful. This is a nephew who disappeared so long ago, the idea that he could be found today seems difficult for him to imagine. "You know, Madam," the old man suddenly says, "I accompanied my cousin to the morgue in Bihać to identify his son. It was impossible to know. We walked by the corpse several times without recognizing him. He was disfigured, his ears and nose cut off. It was in the summer, the flies were everywhere, swarms of flies, like bees. He too fell into an ambush. He had been sent to the front to bring blankets and food for the troops who were suffering from the cold, so much snow that winter. They took him on the road, they were waiting for him. They killed him and mutilated his face."

"But was it summer or winter?" Darija says, interrupting his account.

"He died in the winter, but his corpse was returned in the summer, in an exchange of bodies."

"Understood. It is very difficult to recognize bodies in those circumstances, when they have been left for several months in the earth. We have realized that many mistakes were made during that time. Some families didn't identify the right body."

"My sister and Semira went to the Bihać morgue, as well.

Semira was still a child, but she was of an age to be able to identify her brother. They did not find him. Maybe he is in the cemetery, in one of those nameless tombs, marked with N.N. Who knows?"

"Regarding the Bihać cemetery, all the N.N. bodies have been exhumed and transferred to the morgues in Šejkovaća or Banja Luka, or their DNA samples have been taken. What this means is if Samir's body has been found, we have his DNA in our database and can identify him."

Darija gets back into her stride, she explains all this as she has countless times before, her voice is convincing and reassuring. She looks at Husnija straight in the eye, using her gaze to oblige him to listen to her and at times she turns towards his spouse to include her in the conversation. "All this... is very difficult..." the old man murmurs. "But what can we do about it? That's how it is and that's it."

"Twenty years ago, the worst happened. What we can do now is try and correct what happened by providing answers."

Husjina concurs with a nod but looks like he does not really believe in these answers. His son has got up to take the coffee off the fire, turn off the gas cooker, prepare the tray with cups, "the ones in in the cupboard, up on the right, where the sugar is," his mother says to him. Then she suddenly turns towards Darija and says: "My son had to wear a cast for a year. He got hit in the leg by a sniper. The bullet went through the muscle and bone, came out the other side."

"No, Mum, they took it out during the operation," the son says, correcting her. He seems a little embarrassed by the situation, having his health issues discussed by his mother. But the mother continues: "Yes, the operation. The worst thing is that it shredded the bone, they had to cut off a bit. One of his legs is shorter by three centimeters now."

"My leg was held together by just flesh and skin," the son explains, taking control of the story. "But the function in the leg came back, I walk practically normally now."

"He has to wear orthopedic soles all the time," the father adds, getting involved in the conversation.

Darija's eyes go back and forth between them, it is difficult to return to the subject of her visit without appearing impolite, when confronted with these parents and their son arguing about who shall be the narrator. She listens, attentive, ready to get the discussion back on the track that led her to this living-room. "They stopped our pension for disability," the son keeps going.

"Oh, really? Seriously?"

"He no longer gets anything." The father persists, "Nor my second son."

"For two years I have been contesting this decision," the son takes up the baton. "But nothing ever happens. This medical commission that gives out certificates for your benefits is a joke. The doctor spends two minutes with you, and that is it. If you pass him a wad, he will sort your papers for you. If you give nothing, you leave empty-handed."

"Yes, the lowlifes are everywhere," Darija admits.

"It is a country of con artists!" the father suddenly says.

"No, it is not a country of con artists, it is a country led by con artists," the son says, correcting him.

Suddenly the discussion gets carried away, the father and son interrupting each other, "Yes, all con artists—but at least in times of peace they could have governed the country with fairness, but oh no, they steal, they lie, they have no shame in front of honest citizens, who struggle, they're all the same Izetbegović, Čović, Dodik, all the same gang in the end," The son is getting on a roll, "Last night, yet another one of them was swaggering away on the TV, talking about former soldiers, what an idiot."

The father looks at me out of the corner of his eye and interrupts his son, addressing Darija.

"Which TV channel did you say she worked for?" He asks, concerned that the discussion does not get too out of hand in front of the camera.

"It's not a TV channel, she is independent," Darija explains, seizing the moment to change the course of the discussion. "As I said to you over the phone, she is making a documentary on our relatives who disappeared during the war, about all these bones still lying waiting in the morgue. She already accompanied me last year on the ground."

The father nods, Darija persists: "It's important the world sees this. I have been doing this work for sixteen years and not once did a journalist search me out in order to tell the story of what the families lived through."

Thanks to the gesturing towards my camera and my few words of Serbo-Croatian, I understand that they are talking about my film, but I don't understand more than that. What I do manage to grasp is how Darija's face turns to each of these three people, the mother's tired eyes behind her glasses, the son's tense expression, the bald father in profile. I hear them finishing each other's phrases, interrupting each other, they have such a need to talk, all three of them, as if they have waited a long time for this visit, to let it all out at once, everything that they have endured, all the pent-up bitterness over the years.

"You work in which region?" The son enquires.

"It's so vast, I cover the whole of the Bosanska Krajina region and a part of Herzegovina. I am on the road every day, here today, tomorrow another place..."

"Do you see the forest up there?" The son says, interrupting her. "That is where the front line was, they shot at us with cannons, mortar bombs, they had a complete view of the town. That is where the snipers were posted."

"We had to do everything at night," adds the father. "Harvest the fields, gather the straw... It was too dangerous during the day. One time, I heard a bullet whistle by my head. He had aimed at me from above. And now we have Dodik saying none of this ever happened, denying the genocide in Srebrenica."

"It is the people's fault," the son interrupts.

"But the people can do nothing!" The father says, getting annoyed. "What are they supposed to do?"

"In two years' time, it's the elections, Papa."

It is impossible for Darija to regain control of the discussion. Fortunately, there is the coffee to be served, the cream-laden cake to eat. I sit next to Darija, I smile at the woman who makes me think of my grandmother. She too used to talk of the war, the one that Finland led against Russia, at Germany's side. During lessons in high school, it was presented to us as a patriotic and defensive war, its veterans celebrated as the heroes of independence. No one talked about the Finnish soldiers who went off to join the ranks of the Nazis, the Jews taking refuge in Finland who were denounced and deported. From this period, my grandmother retained a visceral hate of Russians whom she could only talk about using insulting words in Finnish, "ryssä," instead of "venäläinen"— as you find here, when some say "tchetnik" instead of "Serb".

My grandmother had met her husband during this time, when he was a young soldier. The only time that she talked to me about this grandfather whom I never got a chance to know, was to explain to me that the war had made him paranoid, he looked for his wife's lovers in the cupboards of the house. Perhaps she told me other things, but that was the story that stayed with me: my grandaddy opening and closing cupboards in the house, trying to flush out an imaginary lover.

I smile at the woman in the scarf, my mouth full of cream cake. My grandmother also had a bitterness inside whose source I could never fathom, perhaps it was just the wounds of life that never quite healed, the injustices that she chose to endure without a word."Do you want milk, Mum?"

"Yes, a little milk."

"I'll let you put in the sugar," the son says to Darija.

"Thanks, just a little sugar for me, so my life is not too bitter," she replies.

I would discover the expression reading Zoran's translation several weeks later. I wondered if Darija had chosen it deliberately on that day.

"It's good, what you are doing," says the son, "it's a good thing, but it's also sad."

"This whole thing is difficult, yes," Darija responds. "But I am pleased when I can bring answers to families. With each identification, I think to myself that I have done the best I can to ensure families have a right to the truth."

"It's difficult to find people now," Husjina carries on. "This is done now, all this."

He still seems doubtful, as if Darija's words do not concern him, as if this whole affair has been over for a long time, as if all these new endeavors do not resolve the uncertainty but on the contrary, awaken it, when he thought it was all settled.

"Anything is possible," Darija insists. "You saw what happened near Prijedor three years ago? We found hundreds of bodies at the Tomašića mass grave, even though they had been buried for more than twenty years... "

"I worked at Tomašića," the father says, interrupting her again. "I was a truck driver around that way, I transported ore to the processing plant, eight kilometers away. I recognized the place on TV. There was a large pit where they extracted the ore. We would circle around the sides of it with the trucks to get to the back of the quarry. That is where they threw in the people afterwards."

"That's right. They brought the bodies in trucks which they emptied into the pit. I went there. The bodies that they brought out were very well preserved because of the clay."

I drink my black coffee, I understand that they are talking about Tomašića. I think to myself that I will never forget the images that I have taken, I carry them inside me now, associated forever with this country. I go back behind the camera, I watch this utterly ordinary scene: elderly parents, their fifty-something son and a guest sitting around with coffee and some cream cake. The discussion continues, like a background noise that I cannot follow, other than to occasionally grasp a few words: Darija saying she is from Banja Luka, that her mother is Croat, her father Serb, the political parties, the TV, the army, Yugoslavia, the people, the politics, always the politics. As if all three of them want to delay the moment when they must confront why Darija has come. As if it frightens them.

"Right, Husjina, we are going to fill in the form together. I have already done it with Semira and I am now going to do it with you." We have already been here an hour.

"What about your cake?"

"No thank you, I really cannot eat any cake, the coffee is enough. I haven't touched it, someone else can eat it."

"A banana, then?"

"The banana will be for the road. Right, Husjina, the actual name of Semir's father is Sulejman, correct? And his mother, meaning your sister, is Haseda?"

The litany of questions begins. As Darija works through her form with Husjina, his wife's gaze becomes increasingly anxious, she wrings her hands.

"Who's there?" she suddenly asks, hearing a sound outside.

"It's nothing, Mum. No one's there."

She cannot calm down, gets up with a struggle using her cane, waves a hand in front of her face. "The flies, what are they all doing here, the flies."

She walks towards the window, each step is painful.

"Leave it, we will deal with it later," her son intervenes.

"No, I am going to get rid of the fly." She manages to get to the window and opens it wide, letting in a breeze of fresh air, and getting rid of a fly that only she can see. I hear Darija's questions coming thick and fast, the clothes, the date of the disappearance, the other family members. Later on, reading the translation rushes, I happen upon this phrase from the woman: "It is hard for a mother to see her children leave to go to war. I have two sons, they both had to go."

"I wanted to show you something," Darija says once we are in the car on the way back, two hours later. "A place I really like. I am so happy to come here with you so that I could show it to you."

"What is it?"

"Some ancient ruins, you'll see."

Our car climbs the road that winds upwards, we turn off, head towards the cliff. At the end of a gravel drive, there is a castle. It looks straight out of a child's fairy tale, with turrets, a window over the entrance arch, part castle for a princess and part vampire's abode. "Come," Darija suddenly says. I follow her into its interior, water runs down the walls and drips onto the stone floor, a ceiling has collapsed. I walk along corridors with flaking paint, I enter into rooms in ruins, the walls have scribblings, names, little and big hearts, one with a date, "4.10.09," another written in red paint, "Dijana + Alen." I walk behind Darija in this place that seems outside of time, she explains to me that the oldest parts of the castle date to medieval times. That it has seen the Ottomans pass through, then the Austro-Hungarians, followed by the period of Yugoslavia. All of the country's history is condensed in these walls that Dijana, Alen and the rest have decided to claim for themselves. It is all there.

"I understand why you like this place," I say.

Darija smiles at me, leads me outside towards the edge of the cliff, where a magnificent view opens out onto the canyon, with fir trees clinging to the slopes, a turquoise river flowing at its bottom, snow on the high plateau opposite, and further away the mountains. She walks towards the low wall that borders the castle. "Come, the view is even more beautiful from here," she calls out to me.

I don't dare tell her that I have vertigo and am scared that I will fall. I keep quiet and grab the tripod with the camera fastened atop it, I climb, my legs shaking. Darija positions herself in front of me, the canyon at her feet, her face radiant. I frame her silhouette against this landscape more ancient than the castle, a landscape from the time before men.

13

IZA'S SON

Darija brakes at my request, then she suggests. "Do you want a view of the snowy valley? Because we are going to go up a little further, there is a place that is more wide open."

"OK, that's good for me." She accelerates again, the car climbs. Generally, I do not like it when someone makes a decision for me, but I am beginning to trust Darjia's eye. She observes me at least as much as I do her through my lens. Sometimes, she asks me questions about how I imagine the film. I talk about the faces of the people we meet, the magnificent landscapes turned into a theater of horror. Talking about the film with her is a way for us to look at the whole of the story that I am weaving and in which she is now becoming the main character.

"Does this work for you, here?" We have arrived on a high

plateau, with a little valley ahead of us. The snow has blanketed everything in white, only the road remains clear, from the passage of cars and trucks across the mountains. I get out the tripod and camera, she uses the time to roll a cigarette, next to the car stopped by the roadside. I frame the horizon and the snow in front of us, and I end up turning the camera towards her, her silhouette and blonde hair in a long red down jacket standing out against the surrounding whiteness, the cigarette, the sunglasses. This is how I see her: alone and determined in the middle of nowhere, going from one house to the next, marking the time with a break long enough for a smoke. She stubs out the butt, turns to face me, and with the lens turned right on her, she smiles, gets out her phone from her pocket and snaps me. "I got you!"

Iza was waiting for us. We have barely sat ourselves down in the sitting room when she launches in with a question; "Why is it that you are interested in my DNA now?" Sitting on a sofa opposite this woman in her sixties, Darija takes a deep breath before answering. She has placed her red plastic sleeve on the low table, leans slightly towards Iza, looking her straight in the eye. I recognize this posture which means: "time for business."

"A few years ago, you gave your blood in order to identify your father, is that correct?"

"Yes, that's right, I gave my blood and my brother Rufad also."

Rufad has just arrived and is now sitting at the other end of the living-room. He has taken off his shoes but not his jacket, as if he is not going to stay. He looks much younger than Iza, whose face has deep wrinkles. He has the same smile as his sister, a smile that goes all the way up to his eyes, suddenly lights them up.

"I am going to explain how it works," Darija continues. "All the blood samples that we receive are automatically compared with the bone samples that we already have in our database. It has turned out that the blood we took from you matches a bone sample. And we know that it cannot be your father's. As a consequence, we have checked if other people in your family have disappeared, or if someone who disappeared was identified using the traditional methods, meaning without DNA analysis. That would mean an error could have taken place during identification."

Darija takes a deep breath. Iza's face has frozen.

"We are discovering this kind of mistake often lately. You have been through this process, you know how grueling it can be. I don't know in what circumstances you recognized your son Ismet, if it was though clothes or identity documents..."

"Perhaps they did not put the right body in the coffin," Iza says interrupting, as if she has thought it through very quickly, to find the explanation. "Maybe they made a mistake at that moment."

"He was exhumed from the Lanište mass grave in 1997, right?"

"Yes, that's it. I have the photos. Rufad, can you pass them to me? They are in the envelope, over there on the table, by the entrance."

She nods at him, Rufad stands up to get the envelope, holds it out to Darija who takes out the photos. It is a pile of color prints, postcard-sized, as they were before digital cameras had yet to arrive, and photos were kept in albums, sorted, arranged and affixed.

"This here, is it the mass grave where they found bodies?" Darija asks.

"Yes."

"Were you there to identify your son?"

"Not me, no... it was my husband."

"Later on, did you recognize any of the objects in the photos? For example, the clothes?"

"My husband said that he recognized it all, the belt, the T-shirt, the fingers, the nails, my son's teeth. He had had them fixed in Austria."

Darija flicks through the pile, slides one photo over another. Bodies lined up next to each other, in a sports hall with a green ground sheet, basketball nets on the walls. The corpse identified as Ismet's is photographed in close-up. Nothing much remains of his face, just a black mass without contours.

"My husband said that it matched him," Iza repeats.

"It is important to know that these identifications are never one hundred per cent certain," Darija continues. "We would not have triggered this new procedure if we did not have concrete proof that shows an error was committed. Either at the point of identification, or when the body was laid in the coffin."

Iza listens in silence, her face no longer expressing anything, not stupefaction, not sadness, just this blankness that makes me think of the faces of the relatives arriving at Tomašića, as if she has just been propelled into the past, at the moment of her child's death. Darija does not allow the silence to dominate, she keeps going.

"I am going to fill in the form, with information regarding your son. He will then be declared as a missing person. And then we can officially undertake all the analyses necessary to repair this mistake."

Darija gets out her documents, begins the litany of questions without any more delay, Waiting does not help, will not rid Iza of the pain that has been awakened.

"Ismet was born the 5th of August 1970, correct?"

"Yes, that is right"

"Here in Biljani?"

"Yes."

"He was not married."

"No."

"And you lived in Biljani at the time?"

"Yes."

"Tell me, what was Ismet's height? Was he tall?"

"About six-two."

"A tall young man, then. Was he thin or fat?"

"Average."

Iza's answers are brief, taciturn and Darija is working through them fast, as if she too wants it done quickly. "Was Ismet right or left-handed?"

"Right-handed."

"What color was his hair?"

"Take a look at me," Rufad says, intervening in the conversation for the first time. He has a broad smile.

"Yes, take a look at him," Iza repeats his words, and the same smile suddenly illuminates her face.

"There is a photo of him over there," Rufad adds, pointing to the bookshelf at the other end of the sitting room.

In the middle of the portraits of two little boys, there is one of a young man with chestnut brown hair and a gentle gaze, a nicely shaped mouth, a black t-shirt, white shirt, denim jacket.

"It's true that you two look like each other," Darija says. "Dark chestnut brown hair then. Did he have that haircut when he disappeared?"

"Yes."

"Do you remember the clothes he was wearing the day of his disappearance? A pair of jeans?"

"Yes, jeans. And some long underwear. Mirsad told me that he never wore that kind of thing, but I myself told him: of course, he did, he slept outside at night. He had taken a bath, he had pulled on Mirsad's underwear. He told me that he recognized everything, the fingers, the belt, the T-shirt."

"I imagine that the belt was leather?"

"Yes."

"And the shoes? What did he have on his feet?"

"I don't know. Maybe sneakers."

"Did Ismet have any illnesses of any kind? Had he had any surgery?"

"No, not at all! He was enrolled in sports college. He was a young man in good health. He was twenty-one years old, a wonderful age to be."

Iza's last sentence is more like a whisper. Behind the camera, I think: She has lived longer with the absence of her son than with him.

"And as well as your father and son, have you lost any other relatives, Iza?"Darija continues.

"My uncle. And several cousins."

Darija notes it all down, ticks the boxes, reviews all the living relatives, particularly the men, on Ismet's father side. They are the ones who transmit the Y chromosome, which makes the research easier. But so little of the men are left. This country is populated with the ghost of sons, brothers, and fathers.

"If I had not done the blood test for dad, we would have never realized any of this," Iza says suddenly, once the documents have been signed. Is it a regret or a simple observation? Would she have preferred to continue to cry at the grave of an unknown, believing he was her son?

"It's true," Darija says. "But it's a good thing that we are taking these steps, because the body that you have buried is almost certainly being searched for by another family."

"Yes, of course." Iza nods her head. "Well, thank you in

any case for dealing with this," she says, clasping her hands on her knees.

"I am the one to thank you. I hope we can fix this mistake as quickly as possible."

Silence descends on the sitting room. The form has been filled, it is time to leave.

"Would you like to drink something? Rufad has brought some wine, it is home-made."

""A little glass then, just to taste it. I am driving."

"And your colleague? It's not like French wine but it's still good."

I take the glass held out to me, I smile. Darija looks for her tobacco pouch, forgotten in the car. "I roll my cigarettes as well," says Iza, laughing and goes to get her reserves, a plastic box filled with pre-rolled cigarettes.

"Home-made roll-ups!" Darija says, joking.

The atmosphere has relaxed in the house, it does good for everyone to laugh a bit. Rufad does not want anything, neither cigarettes or wine, and Iza makes fun of him: "It is only the women who drink and smoke here!"

I can grasp the meaning of her sentence thanks to a few familiar words, žene, vino, cigareta, and I laugh as well. I think of all the cigarettes, in so many cafés, all the glasses of rakija, beer, and cherry liqueur that I have shared with these women in this country, ever since I have been coming here; I think of these female survivors who still make the food, look after the children who survived and the ones that they have given birth to since; I think of the women who knit the woollen socks, who smoke and drink, clinking their glasses together, who gulp down tranquilizers to see off the nightmares and antidepressants to shield themselves from memories too hard to bear; all those who continue to take care of a husband whom the war destroyed, who endure the absence of the missing, who wait the accepted time before remarrying because trying to find happiness too quickly is not the done thing, but to remain alone is hard to endure as well. Strong women who tell their children about the father who is no longer, or the lost cousin, women who tell the story because their children must know, who remain silent to protect them, who wonder if they should talk about it or not, or how to know what is right.

The wine is zesty and fizzy, Rufad asks me what I think, I say that I like it a lot, I smile, Darija translates. On the shelf, the frame of the portrait of Ismet is pink like Iza's sweater, a soft warm pink. There is the word for widow, for orphan, but the mother who lives with absence of her son, there is nothing, no words, as if man cannot formulate them.

Once we're back in the car, I ask Darija, "How many cases are like this, like Iza's?"

"We estimate seven thousand traditional identifications took place. Generally, they are done on the basis of the clothes. The mothers often talk about woollen socks or sweaters that they knitted for their sons, that kind of detail. But the problem is, it is just clothes, they are interchangeable. For example, this happened in the Srebrenica siege. The clothes of those who died during the siege were possibly taken by others. How to know? Even identity documents in a pocket mean nothing. That is why we have decided to verify each case from now on."

"But it is a massive amount of work!"

"Yes, especially as you need on average three blood samples in order to determine identity. That is more than 20,000 samples… How do you find people twenty years afterwards, when families believe they have dealt with it?"

"Is this what you are going to work on now?"

"Yes, well it depends actually. The project will have to be first accepted by the associations for the families of the missing and that is not a given. They understand the point of it but it is very complicated for the people who have already buried their relatives. I understand them. Honestly, I think that some of them would rather just continue to live without knowing the truth... For now, we're not contacting the families other than in cases like Iza's, where we have a match with an existing sample—meaning we have a body waiting somewhere, because we don't want to leave people with an empty grave. But if we get this project going, the idea would be to contact everyone..."

Then she adds, with note of worry in her voice: "It's important that they don't question my job, because if I find out in a few months my job is going the way of my lab colleague's ones..."

The silence fills the car.

"When will you know?"

"Between now and the end of the year, I hope. Hey, we could take another way back. We won't be far from Sanski Most, we could stop to say hi to Ajša, in Šejkovaća. Would that be OK?"

"Of course, it will be great to see them again."

"Perfect! And when we leave from there, we can stop to eat a trahana at Stara Bašta in Kozarac."

I do not discuss it too much. Darija has her habits on every route; her cafés, her restaurants with a preferred dish, her places to smoke a cigarette. The day before, I told her jokingly that if she ever changed job, she could be a tourist guide. She knows this region inside out. She replied with a satisfied smile that I was not the first to say it.

In Šejkovaća, Ajša welcomes us with Nescafe, as usual. She is happy to see us, it has made her day, she says. Of the team that I knew, only she and Samir, the policeman who guarded the site, remain in the little prefab. Ajša is about to leave, she as well. She wants to join her husband in Germany, have more work opportunities, a decent salary and a simpler life. Given the cuts on the ICMP's activities in the country, it seems better to go and find one's happiness elsewhere.

"Do you think I can go into the hangar?" I ask Ajša.

"Yes, of course. Hang on, I am just going to call the prosecutor to check if you can enter with your camera." She makes her call, tells me that it is OK.

I push open the door, alone, with my camera. It is the sixth time that I have come here. I allow my eyes to take in the full space that I know by heart. The photos on the wall, the rows of trolleys, the tables. This time, there are eight of them, lined side by side in the middle of the large room. On each of them, the bones have been laid out to recreate a body. At the foot of each table, sits a pile of washed and folded clothes, the personal effects placed atop them: a watch, a razor, a button found in a pocket. I look at all these remains, and, for the first time, I see the contours of a life. Next to a pair of jeans and a striped shirt, a brown leather belt has been rolled up.

At the Stara Bašta restaurant in Korazac, our plates of trahana in front of us—a soup with homemade pasta into which thick slices of white bread are dipped—Darija suddenly asks me why I got interested in all this. Where did I get the idea from, why the missing? I tell the story, from the beginning, right from its very inception six years ago. I recount how I followed Senem into the hangar at Šejkovaća for the first time, to what extent I had no idea about any of this. I tell her about my encounters in Trnopolje, all the stories haunted by the missing, who can neither be held onto nor let go. I tell her about the week that I spent in the mass grave at Tomašića, the bodies that came out of the earth, the look in the eyes of the relatives when they came to see it, their eyes filled with hope, which, once on the site, went completely empty, as if the massacre has just happened. I tell her about my six-year journey to these strange places, where there is what the psychologists designate in poetic terms as 'ambiguous loss' and that Suada, a mother of two missing sons, explained it to me this way: "I don't know where they are. They are neither in the land of the living or the dead."

"This is where I am," I conclude. "It is because of all these things that I want to make the film. Because I think it is important to tell this story."

I see the emotion in her eyes. We finish our soup, we drink a coffee, she rolls a cigarette and we get back on the road, on the way to another house.

2020

14

THE CIRCLE

O n the computer screen, Senem is looking at me with a wide smile and tired eyes. It is late in Soukhoumi, in the self-proclaimed state of Abkhazia, and she has just been on the road for six hours.

"Taina, you haven't changed!"

"Yes, I have," I protest, laughing, "Have you seen my grey hair! I did not have it before."

"And me, I have less and less hair" she retorts, laughing too.

I recognize her voice, her determined gaze, that gaze that is sometimes unflinching.

It has been more than five years since we last met. Ever since we said goodbye at Šejkovača in 2015, we had exchanged a few messages, sent each other our news now and then. I have had the time to finish my film. It took four years to be financed, filmed and edited, and was ready to be shown when the pandemic closed cinemas and borders in the spring, preventing Darija from coming to Paris for the preview or my going to Bosnia, confining us all to the parameters of our personal screens. I had sent Senem a link to the film so she could discover the story that had begun with her: "Well done," she had written to me. Knowing her taste for a job accomplished properly, I appreciated the compliment.

"I often thought of you when I first arrived here, three months ago," she tells me.

"Really?"

"This country makes me think of Bosnia. It is as if I am rediscovering my own country, but through the eyes of someone who does not know it. I thought to myself that it must have been like this for you, when you first came."

Her words touch me. She knows the journey that I have taken since we first met in the trailer at Šejkovača, one misty morning in September, ten years ago. I will have to ask her why she decided to put her trust in me that day.

"Before taking up this post, I was asking myself a lot about what I wanted," she says. After the posting in Baghdad, I felt the need to come back to a normal life. And then this position opened up. I said to myself: 'That's for me.' And I was right."

It has been five years since Senem left her country, first for Afghanistan, then Iraq, and now the Republic of Georgia. Her fifteen years spent working on mass graves and in the Bosnian morgues have made her a specialist much sought after by the ICRC, the International Committee of the Red Cross. She has become a forensics expert, the term that that they like to use in the world of international organizations, this world of expatriates who move from one conflict zone to another.

"At the start, in Kabul, I thought a lot about Bosnia, for the first months, I could not stop wondering whether I was abandoning the families."

Then it passed. The work took over as it always does. She learned to live with the guilt pangs of the ones who left— perhaps she also learnt to put her trust in the ones who continued the work after her, and accepted the idea that she was not irreplaceable. She said that once she had got through the doubts of the first months, the country captivated her, taught her a huge amount. With her team, she was given the responsibility of devising a "a plan for managing corpses" with the authorities, to ensure that bodies could be easily returned to families, even in conflict situations.

Senem calls this prevention: ensuring bodies do not become the missing. For someone like her accustomed to mass graves dug in remote parts of Bosnia, the approach was surprising: the bodies were not hidden to conceal the crime here. Her role was not about convincing the actors in the conflict of the necessity to hand back bodies to their relatives, but simply organizing their return.

"For me, this was completely new: in this country sapped by war and where serious numbers of people die each day, certain values had been preserved, and shared."

Everything rested on one point of agreement: an enemy was still a human being, and his corpse should be returned to his family for a dignified burial.

I think of the first bodies that I saw in Šejkovaća ten years ago when Senem explained their position in the pit to me— carefully lined up, faces towards the sky —and what she could deduce from this: the gravedigger could not have been the murderer. When one has killed, one doesn't take such care with the bodies.

Over there, in Kabul, she had understood that it was possible to kill one's enemy without forgetting the respect due his corpse. Was that perhaps the difference between war and genocide? She talked to me about all this, and I heard surprise in her voice. She said that she had never considered that the relationship to the dead could be so different. I wondered if this observation had not accentuated for her the horror of her work in Bosnia, where the bodies had been spread between primary and secondary mass graves, and how the dead were mistreated to conceal the crimes. I had wanted to ask her the question, but did not interrupt her, she had gone off into her memories, her eyes at times darting sideways as she searched for the right words.

"Then three days before the end of my posting, my colleague was assassinated."

The sentence is brutal. The team knew that this could happen. During the twenty months that Senem spent in Kabul, six other staff of the ICRC and the Red Cross were killed. But her colleague Lorena, a Spanish physiotherapist, was also a friend. Senem tells me: repatriating the body, meeting the family... For the first time, she had to deal with the body of someone close to her. "Back in Sarajevo, I didn't speak to anyone for two weeks," she said.

Once again, it was Darija who had comforted her. They went away on holiday to their little island off Croatia, as usual. The words came back, and with them questions about what she would do next, Senem had said to herself she would never go away again, but back from holiday, a week at home convinced her of the opposite.

"I got bored," she says. "So, I applied for Baghdad, and they accepted me."

I listen to her talking from her hotel room in Soukhoumi, and it feels like we are continuing a conversation started the day before, as if we were still in Šejkovaća. She talks to me about Iraq, "a whole other story," and evokes a sinister picture in a simple preamble: end of the Islamic State's reign, massive humanitarian needs, human rights utterly ignored. "For us, we must help with the setting up of a national research project on the missing." Hearing her enthusiastic tone, I understand the situation that she has described is above all an exciting challenge to her. She talks to me about her three years spent in Baghdad using abstract terms: systemic approach, reinforcing capacity, recommended norms, focal points. I recognize the technocratic language of international organizations.

"But who actually were you working with? With the authorities, with civil society?"

"With everybody. The authorities, the family associations, the human rights organizations, the professionals... I made sure that all of them built a system together that worked." She is proud of the mechanism that she managed to put in place, even if it is still fragile. "I did not resolve one single identification case during those three years, but I know that it is possible to establish hundreds now."

She talks, puffing on her electronic cigarette. She gets up to open the window, keeping the phone in her hand, her screen swirls and shakes before stabilizing again when she collapses on the bed, her head propped against a wall with pale wallpaper decorated with bright patterns. She has dark rings around her eyes, it cannot be far from midnight over there.

"Here in Georgia, it's like in Bosnia," she says. Her face disappears behind a cloud of vape smoke. "We do everything here, we exhume, we examine, we identify, we return the bodies to the families. The only thing we do not do ourselves, are the DNA analyses, which are done by an independent outside laboratory."

"But are you in Georgia or Abkhazia?"

"Both. I am based in Tbilisi, the Georgian capital, but I act across the whole territory, including the Abkhazia and South Ossetia regions, affected by war. Lots of people disappeared. Do you now the history of these parts?"

"No, not a lot."

"Look on the internet, I'm sure it will interest you. It often reminds me of Prijedor. In fact, it is as if this place was made for me. It is like closing the circle."

Her sentence makes me smile. I think of all the discussions that I have had with her over the last ten years, and all of the ones with Darija for six years, the fact that I know both of them well despite the fact that we have never been all three together, save the one time when Darija came to pick me up in Šejkovaća, for a first day of filming with her, and we had a quick coffee in the trailer before heading off. I had filmed them talking. I think of the friendship that links us all, me in Paris, Darija from the road in Krajina in Bosnia, Senem from one conflict zone to another on the edges of Asia and Europe. I think of the stories entrusted to us, to which we try to give a meaning, Darija from four drops of blood and the stories that she hears, Senem with the bones that she manipulates with her hands, and myself with the stories that I weave together.

"I don't know which direction my career will take next," Senem continues. "But for now, it would be hard for me to be happier in a job than I am now."

Her image freezes, then disappears. We have lost the connection. All I can see is Senem's profile photo, a little ICRC flag at half-mast. She changed it the day her colleague in Mazar-i-Sharif died three years ago and has never changed it since.

An hour later, I receive a message; "I'm sorry, no more internet. I was so happy to be able to talk to you. Goodnight!"

"Good night," I reply. "We can pick up again another night".

"Yes, let's do that."

I type Abkhazia into a search engine and start to read.

MERCI*
HVALA

For your never-failing trust in me on each of my trips over the last ten years:

Senem Škulj

Darija Vujinović

Sudbin Musić

Ervin Blažević aka Švabo

Zoran Vučić

All the KIP team, in Šejkovaća, and in particular:

Ajša Smalić, Asmir Hodžić, Zlatan Musić, Bejsa Crljenković, Samir Selman as well the NN Team in Visoko and in East Sarajevo.

In Trnopolje, hvala puno:

Mirela Maroslić, without your words, this story would have never begun, Mehmed and Emira Maroslić, my family in Bosnia, for your constant warm welcome.

Rasma Hodžić, for your vegetables, your coffee and your stories in your Barbie house.

In Paris, thank you:

Julie Biro, for your anecdotes, which led me there for the very first time and the return journey through the Balkans, the year a volcano exploded and grounded the planes.

Zabou Carrière, my precious colleague on the road with whom I first set foot in Prijedor, Kozarac, Šejkovaća and Tomašića, thank you for your images which helped me tell this story, ten years later.

Jacques Deschamps, for your description of two living women which sparked this film, Chantal Richard, for having noticed my black notebooks and never letting them go, Clémence Billault and Cyril Gay, for having guessed there was a story even before I began to tell it.

And to you, whom I owe a red rose from Emira's garden, thank you for the countless times you read this book, for the joy and light that you bring into my life, even when it is filled with the dead and the missing, from one year to the next.

AUTHOR BIO

Born in Senegal in 1973, Taina Tervonen is a Finnish journalist, filmmaker and author writing in French and currently based in Paris. Self-described as a "teller of true stories", she is the author of several books of non-fiction that deal with serious social topics. Her work, "The Country of the Disappeared" was the winner of the 2019 Louise Weiss Prize for European Journalism, and her film "Speaking with the Dead" was her first full-length feature documentary and a selection of the Cinéma du Réel festival in 2020. She is the recipient of the Jan Michalski Award in 2022 for this title, originally published as "Les Fossoyeuses" (Editions Marchialy) in 2021, which celebrates a work of excellence by a European writer that concerns human rights. Her most recent work, "Les Otages" (*Hostages*), will be published by Schaffner Press in 2025 in an English translation by Sara Hanaburgh.

TRANSLATOR BIO

Sarah Robertson is an independent translator based in the UK, who has worked on a broad range of book projects from travel, to art and architecture. She lives in London.